MOTHER SHIPTON'S PROPHECIES

Mother Shipton's Prophecies

THE EARLIEST EDITIONS

With an Introduction

GEORGE MANN · MAIDSTONE

MOTHER SHIPTON'S PROPHECIES

First published in the United Kingdom 1881

First published in this edition 1978

This edition copyright © George Mann Books, 1978

ISBN 0 7041 0062 2

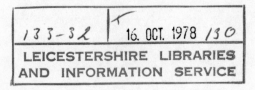
Printed in Great Britain by
Biddles Ltd, Guildford, Surrey
for George Mann Books, P.O. Box 22
Maidstone, in the County of Kent

MOTHER SHIPTON:

A COLLECTION OF THE

EARLIEST EDITIONS OF HER
PROPHECIES.

——-

I.—PROPHECIES OF MOTHER SHIPTON,
1641.

II.—STRANGE & WONDERFUL HISTORY
OF MOTHER SHIPTON, 1686.

III.—LIFE AND DEATH OF MOTHER
SHIPTON, 1684.

——

WITH AN INTRODUCTION.

——

MANCHESTER :
ABEL HEYWOOD & SON, 56 & 58, OLDHAM STREET.

CONTENTS.

—

MOTHER SHIPTON (from the Prophecies, 1686).

INTRODUCTION.

YORKSHIRE has produced many notable men and women, but it may be doubted if any of them have ever attained the persistent and world-wide fame of Mother Shipton. For one hundred and forty years edition after edition has been issued from the press of her oracular sayings. Her name has become familiar in our mouths as household words, and yet if we ask, in the critical spirit of the modern time, it must be admitted that History is silent respecting her, and that all we have to depend upon is the vague voice of Tradition. The date of her birth is stated by one account to have been 1486 or 1488, whilst another account says that she died in 1651, at the age of seventy! No record of her existence appeared in print until a century and a half after the supposed date of her entrance into this world. The scanty references to her in the works of the historians of Yorkshire are all evidently based upon local traditions or on the pamphlets issued in the seventeenth century. Hargrove and Allen state that she was born in 1488, near the Dropping Well and Knaresborough, and that her prophecies had been preserved in MS. in Lord P——'s family.* These pamphlets do not give us any great clue as to the individuality of the prophetess. Much in them is purely imaginative, and only interesting as a specimen of the grotesque in popular literature. As there is proverbially fire where there is smoke, we may, perhaps, assume that some sybil living by the Dropping Well at Knaresborough acquired a reputation for foreseeing the future, and that her dark sayings were repeated from mouth to mouth until some lucky wight, perhaps a Londoner brought northwards by the royal progresses which preceded the civil war, bethought him of com-

---

* Probably Lord Powis. In Sloane, MS. 647—4, fol. 89, there is a piece entitled, " A Prophecy found in ye manuscript in ye year 1620." A woman born in 1488 would, however, scarcely be capable of prophesying mundane events in 1620. The MS. contains no name, but the verses have been given as a prediction of Mother Shipton's, coupled with a statement that she died in 1651, when she was over seventy. There is a discrepancy of more than a century in the two dates given for her birth. (See *Oddfellows' Magazine*, July, 1881, p. 168.)

mitting them to print. This was in 1641, and in 1645 they were reprinted by the famous William Lilly, who was a firm believer in astrology, and collected a number of ancient and modern prophecies. Mr. W. H. Harrison says:—" Line by line I have compared these two earliest versions, and find that they agree tolerably closely. Lilly spells Besley's name 'Beasley.' 'Mungate barre' Lilly spells 'Walmsgate bar,' and rather more of Besley's narrative is set in type in verse. 'Stocknmore' is rendered 'Storktonmore.' Here and there Lilly's version contains trifling additions not in the earlier pamphlet. For instance, it says that after Mother Shipton told Lord Percy that his body would be buried in York pavement and his head carried into France, 'they all laughed, saying that would be a great lap between the Head and the Body.'"

Her fame in the seventeenth century was very great. Pepys, in his diary under date 20th Oct., 1666, writes of Sir Jeremy Smith: " He says he was on board the ' Prince ' when the news came of the burning of London; and all the Prince said was, that now Shipton's prophecy was out."

But if History is silent Tradition has been very busy with her name. Many predictions are attributed to her. A number of these have recently been gathered by Mr. William Grainge, and printed in the *Palatine Note-book* for April, 1881. From this article we take the following:—

Scarcely any event hereabouts of more than ordinary importance can occur but we are gravely told that " Mother Shipton's prophecy has come to pass" therein or thereby. Should the spring be late, the summer be cold, or snow fall earlier than usual, we are at once told that Mother Shipton prophesied that " we should not know winter from summer. except by the leaves on the trees, before the world was at an end." When railways began to spread throughout the country, Mother Shipton had, in the popular belief, foreseen them, and had said—

" When carriages without horses run,
    Old England will be quite undone."

This, like many other equivocal sayings, may be said to be realised in the new state of things which the extension of railways has been the means of introducing into the country; so that *old England* may be said to be *undone* by the rapid growth of *young England*.

When the railway was being made between Harrogate and York, a lofty viaduct was needed to cross the river Nidd at Knaresborough, which was nearly completed, when through some deficiency in the construction the whole fabric fell into the water ! The popular voice at once declared that Mother Shipton had said that " the big brig across the Nidd should tummle doon twice and stand for ivver when built the third time." The second fall and the third building are yet in the future. This prophecy was never heard by anyone until after the catastrophe occurred.

Prophecies of this kind are not confined to the immediate locality where the prophetess was born; they are spread over the country far and wide; and they exist in North-East Lancashire. Our seer predicted that Pickhill, a parish town in the North Riding, would never thrive until a certain family became extinct, and *P'cts*, or Money-hill, an old barrow or burial mound adjoining it, should be cut open. Both these events came to pass; the family indicated became extinct in the year 1850; and Money-hill was cut open, and nearly all removed by the formation of the Leeds Northern Railway in 1851. Will the place thrive better now ?

Another of " Shipton's wife's prophecies" had reference to the Castle Hill at Northallerton, a mound which she declared should be filled with blood. The place has become a cemetery for the burial of the dead, which in a limited sense is a fulfilment of the saying; for we must bear in mind that the utterances of the most gifted seers if tied down to exact literality will often be found wanting.

Another of her predictions was fulfilled at the antique village of Ulleskelfe-on-the-Wharfe. The said village had from time immemorial possessed a large tithe-barn, and a public spring of water called " the Keld." Our prophetess declared that a public road should run through the barn, and the Keld be dried up. No one could believe that such things would happen; tithebarns would exist and water spring for ever. Yet the making of the York and North Midland Railway effected both these seeming impossibilities; the iron roadway was laid directly over the place where the barn had stood, and the Keld was removed to another place.

An unfulfilled prophecy relates to Walkingham Hill. a ridge of high land some three miles northward of Knaresborough. The old dame is reported to have said that a time would come when all the hill would run with blood; but with what kind of blood she said not. If the swarms of rabbits which infest it be meant, the prediction is fulfilled every day.

She is also said to have foreseen the use of the Harrogate waters, the building of that town, and the railway bridges leading to it, and to have given her prescience shape and expression in the following very rude lines which have evidently been made in the neighbourhood, for they bear no signs of Cockney manufacture :—

> " When lords and ladies stinking water soss,
> High brigs o' stean the Nidd sal cross,
> An' a toon be built on Harrogate Moss."

The first and last predictions at one time were not likely to come to pass, if they were really uttered before the events; they are, however, now literally fulfilled. for lords and ladies come from all parts of the kingdom to *drink* (synonymous with *soss*) the strong and *stinking* sulphur waters. Harrogate Moss has been reclaimed from the rude Forest of Knaresborough, of which it formed a part, and one of the most elegant towns in the county of York has been built upon it, entirely through the influence of those stinking waters which persons of high breeding are said to *soss*. Two rather lofty viaducts across the river Nidd conduct the railways from the north and east to the town, and these, we suppose, are the " high brigs o' stean" meant by the prophetess. The highest brig is, however, on the south, across the valley of the Cumple. which is not noticed. This prediction is probably not more than thirty years old.

The latest application of the old sybil's name to a recent event took place last year, 1880, when the village of Fewston, which is built partly upon a moving landslip. gave a slight move, cracking the walls of about a dozen houses from the bottom to the top, and appearing as though it would slide down into one of the large reservoirs which the Leeds Corporation has constructed in the valley of the Washburn for the purpose of supplying that town with water. When the slip took place the credulous and alarmed people (or some of them) declared that Mother Shipton had prophesied that Fewston village should slide into Washburn river before the world was at an end.

Nor are these traditions confined to Yorkshire. In East Norfolk she is made to say :—" The town of Yarmouth shall become a nettle-bush. That the bridge shall be pulled up ; and small vessels sail to Irstead and Barton Roads." Also, " Blessed are they that live near Potter Heigham, and double-blessed them that live in it.*

The Rollwright stones have been associated with the name of Dame Shipton. The local tradition says that a knight, with a small band of followers, meditated the conquest of England, but stayed his progress at the forest near the village of Shipton-under-Whichwood, in order to consult Mother Shipton. A quarrel ensued, and the knight returned in great anger. Next day the band came to a steep ascent, which the knight began to ascend, when the figure of the witch was seen to obstruct his path. " Out of my way, hag," he cried ;

> " If Long Compton I may see,
> Then King of England I shall be."

The witch replied—

> " Rise up Hill, stand fast Stone !
> King of England thou shalt be none !"

At her word the entire array of warriors were transformed to stone.†

In Somerset one of Mother Shipton's prophecies was due to come true on Good Friday of 1879, when Ham Hill was to have been swallowed up by an earthquake, and Yeovil swept by a deluge.

* Harrison : Mother Shipton Investigated, p. 64.
† Household Words, Vol. XIV., 1856, p. 157.

Large numbers went as near as they thought safe, to see it; many of the inhabitants of the threatened district, more consistently with the state of their belief, fled from their homes and took refuge with friends at some distance. As the stroke of twelve approached, when the awful event was to " come off," there was a queer feeling, mixed of terror and unbelief, pervading the air. When all was over, and the clock was silent, and the disappointed crowd had to disperse, there was a better chance for rational faith than there has been in those parts since Mother Shipton's own day.

If asked, "Who was Mother Shipton?" many in reply to such a question would say "A famous prophetess, who foretold the invention of the telegraph, the use of steam, and who declared that the end of the world should be in the year 1881." Copies of this prophecy are freely sold, and contain the following lines :—

> A house of glass shall come to pass
> In England—but alas !
> War will follow with the work
> In the land of the Pagan and Turk ;
> And State and State in fierce strife
> Will seek each others life.
> But when the North shall divide the South,
> An Eagle shall build in the Lion's mouth.
>
> Carriages without horses shall go,
> And accidents fill the world with woe.
> Primrose Hill in London shall be,
> And in its centre a Bishop's See.
>
> Around the world thoughts shall fly,
> In the twinkling of an eye.
>
> Water shall yet more wonders do,
> Now strange, yet shall be true.
> The world upside down shall be ;
> And gold found at the root of tree.

Through hills men shall ride,
And no horse or ass be by his side.
Under water men shall walk,
Shall ride, shall sleep, shall be seen,
In white, in black, in green.

Iron in the water shall float,
As easy as a wooden boat.
Gold shall be found, and found,
In a land that's not now known.
Fire and water shall more wonders do,
England shall at last admit a Jew.
The Jew that was held in scorn
Shall of a Christian be born, and born.

Three times three shall lovely France
Be led to dance a bloody dance,
Before her people shall be free.
Three Tyrant Rulers shall she see;
Three times the People rule alone;
Three times the People's hope is gone;
Three Rulers in succession see,
Each spring from different dynasty.
Then shall the worser fight be done,
England and France shall be as one.

All England's sons that plough the land,
Shall be seen book in hand.
Learning shall so ebb and flow,
The poor shall most wisdom know.

The world to an end shall come
In eighteen hundred and eighty-one.

Mr. Charles Hindley has since confessed that he
fabricated this doggerel in order to sell an edition
of Shipton which he printed in 1862. That Mr.
Hindley was not the first to credit Mother Shipton
with predictions of which she was quite innocent
is evident from an anecdote told by an anony-
mous correspondent of *Notes and Queries*.* He
states that he once called upon John Taylor, the

* 2nd s. xi. 97.

editor of the *Sun*, who exclaimed, "We have them
now, one of their gang (Monument is the fellow's
name) has peached; and he is lodged in the
Tower for safe keeping!" "Ah! ha," was the
reply, "Mother Shipton's prophecy, word for
word!—

> When the monument doth come to the Tower
> Then shall fall Rebellion's power."

The unsuspecting editor put the prophecy into
his paper, whence it was copied by many other
journals. Taylor was, however, so anxious to see
the "original" copy that a confession of the hoax
was the final result.

At one of the debates in the Cambridge Union,
Praed followed a speaker who had indulged in a
vein of gloomy vaticination, and Praed said that
the speech brought to his mind a prophecy of
Mother Shipton, which his facile powers of
versification enabled him to manufacture on
the spot.*

This is by no means a new trick. Throughout
the middle ages prophecies were freely employed
by the different contending parties in order
to strengthen their hold upon the public, and
allusions to accomplished events were freely
interpolated, in order to give greater credit to
prognostications of the future, in which the wish
was father to the thought.

Turning from these modern imitations, let us
now record the gradually increasing literature
that has gathered around the name of Mother
Shipton. The following list, though not com-
plete, will show that much has been written
about her:—

* *Notes and Queries*, 2nd s. xi. 33.

1641.

The Prophesie of Mother Shipton in the Raign of King Henry the Eighth. Foretelling the death of Cardinal Wolsey, the Lord Percy and others, as also what should happen in insuing times. London. Printed for Richard Lownds, at his Shop adjoining to Ludgate, 1641. 4to, 4 leaves, with a cut on the title.

[This is reprinted at p. 1 of the present volume.]

1641.

A True Coppy of Mother Shipton's Last Prophesies : As they were taken from one Joane Waller, in the year of our Lord 1625. Who died in March last 1641. being ninety-four yeares of age. Of whom Mother Shipton had prophesied that she would live to heare of Wars within this Kingdom, but not to see them, &c. London : Printed, for T. V. 1641. 4to., 4 leaves.

1641.

Five Strange and wonderful Prophesies and Predictions of several men foretold long since. All which are likely to come to passe in these our distracted times, viz.

1. Ignatius his prophesie. &c.
2. Some of Scottish Merlins prophesies.
3. Old Ottwell Bins his prophesies.
4. Master Brightman his predictions.
5. Mother Shipton's prophesies more fuller and larger than ever before was printed. 4to. 4 leaves.

1642.

Two strange Prophesies, Predicting wonderfull events to betide this yeere of Danger. in this Clymate, of which some have already come to passe. Well worthy of note : The one being found in the Reigne of King Edward the Fourth : The other in the Reigne of King Henry the Eighth : named Mother Shipton. London, Printed for G. Smith, 1642. 4to. With a wood cut head of Mother Shipton on the title.

1642.

Six strange prophesies predicting wonderful Events to betide these Years of Danger, &c. viz., Mother Shipton's Prophecies, Ignatius Loyolla, Sybilla's Prophecies, 1642. 4to. With a wood cut portrait of Mother Shipton.

1642.

Prophecies, foretelling Wonderful Events to fall out in this Kingdome, viz., Mother Shipton's Prophecies, Merlin's. &c.; whereunto is added strange News from Oundle, in Northamptonshire, 1642. 4to. With a cut.

1645.

A Collection of Ancient and Modern Prophesies. By William Lilly. London, 1645. 4to.

1648.

Twelve strange Prophecies besides Mother Shipton's, predicting wonderful events. Lond. 1648. 4to.

Thirteen strange Prophecies besides Mother Shipton's. Lond. 1648. 4to.

1662-3.

Mother Shipton's Prophecies, with three and xx. more, all most terrible and wonderful, predicting strange Alterations to befall this climate of England. Printed by T. P. for F. Coles. 1663. 4to, with a woodcut on title. In prose and verse.

There was an edition 1662, 4to, with the same woodcut on title. This cut has been copied in Mr. Halliwell's Account of MSS. in the Plymouth Library, 1853.

1667.

Moeder Schipton's Prophecyen van Engelandt. Ofte de Prophecyen van Schiptons Vrouw, gepropheteert in het Jaer 1539, ten tijden van Koningh Henricus den Achsten Koning van Engelandt. * * Uyt het Engelsch overgeset nae de copie van London. In's Gravenhage by Crispijn Hoeckwater. Anno 1667. 4to., pp. 8.

1667.

The Life and Death of Mother Shipton (by R. Head). London, printed for W. Harris, 1667. 4to.

1682.

Forewarn'd, Fore-Arm'd, or England's timely warning in general and London's in particular. By a collection of five prophetical Predictions published by Mr. William Lilly forty years ago; two of Mr. John Gadbury's, anno 1678. And one of Mother Shipton; long since, all at large. London, Printed for John Powel, 1682. 4to, pp. 6.

1684.

The Life and Death of Mother Shipton (by R. Head). London, Printed for Benj. Harris, 1684. 4to.
[This is re-printed at p. 23 of the present volume.]

1686.

The Strange and Wonderful History of Mother Shipton, plainly setting out her prophecy, Birth, Life, Death and Burial, with an excellent collection of all her famous Prophecys more compleat than ever yet before published. Printed for W. H. and sold by J. Conyers in Fetter Lane. 1686. 4to.
[This is re-printed at p. 7 of the present volume.]

1687.

The Life and Death of Mother Shipton (by R. Head). London : Printed for W. Harris, 1687. 4to.

CIRCA 1688.

The Life of Mother Shipton. A new Comedy, as it was acted nineteen days together with great applause. Written by T. T[hompson], London. 4to.

1700.

Mother Shipton's prophesies, with several strange prophesies by Ignatius Sybilla. *(s. l.)* 1700. 8vo.

1797.

Mother Shipton's Life and curious Prophecies. London, 1797. 8vo.

1797.

Wonders ! ! ! past, present, and to come ! being the strange prophecies and uncommon Predictions of the famous Mother Shipton, generally known by the appellation of the Yorkshire Prophetess, copied from the original scroll delivered by her to the Abbot of Beverly : Privately preserved in a noble family for many years, and lately discovered among other curious and valuable manuscripts. London, re-printed for S. Baker. 1797. 12mo, pp. 23.

1797.

Mother Shipton's Legacy, or a favourite Fortune Book, in which is given a pleasant interpretation of Dreams and a collection of prophetical verses. York, 1797.

1797.

The Life and History of the famous Mother Shipton and her daughter Peggy. Collected from the antient Caledonian Chronicle in the Scottish dialect. 2 parts. London, J. Davenport, 1797. 12mo.

CIRCA 1800.

The History of Mother Shipton. Newcastle. 4to. [Circa 1800].

CIRCA 1800.

Strange and Wonderful history and prophecies of Mother Shipton. Printed by M. Randall, Stirling [circa 1800] 12mo

CIRCA 1800.

The History of Mother Shipton. Printed and sold by J. Turner, Coventry [circa 1800]. 8vo, 12 leaves, with cuts.

CIRCA 1800.

History of Mother Shipton, Coventry, n. d. [circa 1800] 12mo.

CIRCA 1800.

The wonderful History and surprising Prophecies of Mother Shipton. Printed and sold by J. Drewery, Derby. 12mo, pp. 23. N. d. [circa 1800.]

CIRCA 1820.

Past, Present, and Future. Fairbairn's edition of the Wonderful Prophecies of the famous Mother Shipton, the Yorkshire Witch. Together with the remarkable Predictions (many of them yet unfulfilled) of Robert Nixon, the Cheshire Prophet. London, J. Fairburn [circa 1820]. 8vo, pp. 24. Price 6d.

CIRCA 1820.

The Life and Death of Mother Shipton (by R. Head) London. 1687. Re-printed by J. Barker, Printer, Great Russel Street, Covent Garden [circa 1820.]

1831.

On a supposed portrait of Mother Shipton. (Gentleman's Magazine, Nov. 1831, vol. ci. pp. 401, 486.)

1851.

The Yorkshire anthology, a collection of ancient and modern ballads, poems, and songs relating to the County of Yorkshire.

London, 1851. 4to. This publication of Mr. J. O. Halliwell included the History of Mother Shipton.

1853.

A Brief Description of the Ancient and Modern MSS., preserved in the Public Library, Plymouth, to which are added some fragments of early literature hitherto unpublished. Edited by James Orchard Halliwell, Esq., F.R.S., F.S.A., Hon. M.R.I.A., Hon. M.R.S.L &c, London, (by C. & J. Adlard) for private circulation only). Contains at p 211 a facsimile of woodcut of Shipton from the Prophecies of 1662.

CIRCA 1860.

The End of the World ! and other remarkable Prophecies by Mother Shipton. together with a sketch of her life, death, and burial. Lond. n. d. [circa 1860.] 8vo. pp. 14.

CIRCA 1860.

Mother Shipton's Wonderful Prophecies. Otley : William Walker, 18mo and 12mo. [circa 1860]. pp. 12.

CIRCA 1860.

Mother Shipton's Fortune-telling book. R. March, Wood bridge-street, London. 4to., pp. 8 [circa 1860.]

1862.

The Life, Prophecies and Death of the famous Mother Shipton. Printed for W. Harris. 1687. Re-printed verbatim 1862 and to be had of the booksellers and all Railway Stations. 12mo. pp. 32. This was got up by Charles Hindley, who garbled it.

1863.

On a portrait of Mother Shipton, presented by Mr. J. O. Halliwell, with remarks by Mr. H. Syer Cuming (Journal of the Archæological Association, 1863).

CIRCA 1868.

Life and Death of Mother Shipton, Knaresboro'. Parr. 8vo.

1869.

The Prophecies of Mother Shipton. London 1641. Facsimile reprint by E. W. Ashbee, F.S.A. London 1869. 4to.

1870.

The Strange and Wonderful History of Mother Shipton,

plainly setting out her prophecy, Birth, Life, Death, and Burial. With an excellent collection of all her famous Prophecys more compleat than ever yet before published. Printed for W. H. and sold by J. Conyers in Fetter Lane. 1686. Reprint by E. Pearson, 1870.

1870.

The Prophecies of Mother Shipton. London 1641. Reprint in the Old Booksellers' Miscellany, edited by Charles Hindley. London, 1870. 8vo.

1878.

The *Shield of Faith*, May, 1878. Contains a notice of the the Hindley prophecy.

1878.

The Life, Death, and Prophecies of Mother Shipton. Extraordinary Revelations by this Wonderful Woman : The End of the World Prophecied ! Also the Prophetic Vision of the Irish Prophet, St. Maol Maodhog O'Morgair, known in his native Irish land as Saint Malachy ; in which is predicted the liberation of Ireland from British Government ! Liverpool. 8vo., pp. 24. The name of the Editor—J. Spybey—is given at p. 21.

1879.

On an Inscribed Stone, at Orchard Wyndham, Somerset, called "Old Mother Shipton's Tomb." With six illustrations. Bristol : William George, 26, Park Street. Taunton : H. Abraham, Fore Street. Williton and Minehead : S. Cox. 1879. 8vo, pp. 32.

CIRCA 1880.

The Remarkable Life of Mother Shipton (of Knaresborough), together with the whole of her remarkable Prophecies. Compiled from many Old and Scarce Works relating to the Celebrated Yorkshire Prophetess. London : Smart and Allen, London House Yard. Leeds : C. H. Johnson, publisher.

1880.

The End of the World in 1881-2, according to Mother Shipton, the Great Pyramid of Ghizeh, and other ancient prophecies relating to Russia and Turkey. London : Houlston & Sons, 1880. 18mo., pp. 116.

1881.

Prophecies of Robert Nixon, Mother Shipton, and Martha the Gipsy. London : Published for the booksellers. [1881.] 12mo. pp. 258.

1881.

Mother Shipton Investigated. The result of critical examination in the British Museum Library, of the literature pertaining to the Yorkshire sybil, by William H. Harrison. London : W. H. Harrison. 1881. 12mo., pp. 64.

1881.

The History and Prophecies of Mother Shipton : Grimsby : M. J. Taylor, 8vo., pp. 24.

1881.

Mother Shipton and her Prophecies (an article signed Isabella Banks in the Girls' Own Paper, May 21, 1881.)

1881.

The Prophecies of Mother Shipton, by Mrs G. Linnæus Banks (*Quarterly Magazine* of the Independent Order of Oddfellows, Jan., 1881.)

1881.

Monsters, by M. D. Conway, B.D., (*Harper's Magazine*, Dec., 1881), with portrait of Mother Shipton.

Articles respecting her have appeared in *Notes and Queries* :—First Series, v., 419. Second Series, xi., 33, 96. Third Series, ix., 139, 229. Fourth Series, i., 139, 491 ; ii., 83, 117, 235 ; iii., 405, 609 ; iv., 213 ; v., 353, 475 ; vii., 25 ; x., 450, 502 ; xi., 60, 207, 355 (at this reference will be found Mr. Hindley's admission that he was the author of Mother Shipton's prediction of the end of the world). Fifth Series, viii., 420.

The earliest edition of Mother Shipton's prophecy is that printed in 1641. It opens in a very abrupt fashion with a statement that she had predicted that Wolsey should never be at York. Drake, the historian of York, says that the Cardinal never came nearer to the city than Cawood, and after a reference to the prophecy adds, " I should not have noticed this idle story, but that it is fresh in the mouths of our country people at this day ; but whether it was a real prediction, or raised after the event, I shall not take upon me to determine. It is more than probable, like all the rest of these kind of tales, the accident gave occasion to the story." After the Wolsey prophecy follow a number of others, some of local and some of general application. Although printed as prose many are in rhyme, and some are certainly of considerable antiquity, having passed current under various other names before they were credited to Mother Shipton. Mr. W. C. Hazlitt mentions another edition published in the same year, which professes to have been taken down in 1625, from the mouth of Jane Waller, who died in March, 1641, at the age of 94, and of whom it is said Mother Shipton had prophesied that she would live to hear of war within the kingdom, but not to see it. This earliest form of the prophecy was several times reprinted, and appears to have whetted the curiosity of the public. To appease the appetite thus created there was published the " Strange and Wonderful History of Mother Shipton," which is reprinted at p. 7. In this tract several local predictions occur, mingled with biographical particulars for which no authority is cited. The subject attracted the attention of Richard Head, a man of more ability than character, and under his facile pen the story expanded into the curious though coarse "Life and Death of Mother Shipton," which is reprinted at p. 23. In this he apologises for the poetic license that has been used, and certainly there is need for his plea. The editions since printed have for the most part been uncritical jumbles of various portions of Head's book and the earlier tracts. They are now carefully reprinted, so that all who are interested may

see what was the original form of the famous
Yorkshire prophecy.*

A word may be said in conclusion as to the
memorials and portraits of Mother Shipton. At
one time a sculptured stone, near Clifton, was
regarded by the people as a monument to Mother
Shipton. In reality it was a mutilated effigy of a
knight in armour, which had probably been taken
from a tomb in St. Mary's Abbey, and set up as a
boundary stone. It is now in the Museum of the
Yorkshire Philosophical Society. †

Still more curious is the monumental mystery
which has been unravelled by Mr. William
George, of Bristol. In Murray's "Somerset,"
under Williton, there is mention of an upright
memorial stone, seven feet high, "sculptured
with a star and female head, and several Roman
letters and numerals, popularly called "Old
Mother Shipton's Tomb.'" This stone faces the
mansion of Orchard-Wyndham, and was supposed
to have been brought from Cumberland, where
the Wyndhams, Earls of Egremont, had property,
and to be identical with a Roman tablet noticed
by Camden. The Williton memorial is elaborately
described in Phelps's "Somerset," under the head
of "Roman Period," a copy of the Latin inscrip-
tion being given, though inaccurately, a qualified
statement which applies also to Dr. Hübner's
learned account of the stone. It now appears
from Mr. George's researches that the tablet
belongs neither to the Cæsars nor to Mother

* Towards the close of the last century appeared a Life and
History of Mother Shipton and her daughter Peggy, in which the
scene is laid at Melross, and a variety of circumstances are
introduced which have no possible connection with the Yorkshire sybil.

† *Notes and Queries.* 4th s., ii., 84.

Shipton, and that it is not the same slab mentioned by Camden, which is smaller, though with similar lettering. In fact, it is a reproduction of the latter stone, but instead of being copied from the original, which probably the sculptor had not access to, it has been transcribed from a very inexact engraving in Gordon's "Itinerarium Septentrionale," the mistakes being faithfully rendered by the copyist. The veritably ancient monument yet exists at Ellenborough, and has recently been engraved in Dr. Collingwood Bruce's "Lapidarium Septentrionale." This spurious stone is shown in the accompanying engraving from the interesting tract by Mr. William George, of Bristol.

"MOTHER SHIPTON'S TOMB" AT ORCHARD-WYNDHAM.
(From Mr. W. George's pamphlet).

In Rackstow's Museum, Fleet-street, London, there was in 1792 " a figure of Mother Shipton, the prophetess, in which the lineaments of extreme old age are strongly and naturally marked. Also her real skull, brought from her burial place at Knaresborough, in Yorkshire."* There was also an effigy of her amongst the waxworks in West-minster Abbey, known to the old-fashioned sight-seers as the " Play of the Dead Volks."† Cuthbert Bede mentions a picture which formerly hung in the large room of the old Crown and Woolpack Inn, on the Great North Road, Conington Lane, near Stilton. It represented a man as the centre of a group of five or six ladies. Labels proceeded from the lips of each. One was, " Oh! mother, I see a man." In the upper left-hand corner was seen the figure of Mother Shipton. The date of the picture was probably about 1750.‖ It was pointed out by Mr. Mortimer Hunt that this exclamation refers to a prophecy not included in the printed books : " The men are to be killed, so that one man shall be left to seven women, and the daughters shall come home and say to their mothers, ' Lawk, mother, I have seen a man.' The women shall have to finish the harvest."‡ This prediction has been given to other modern prophets.

In 1874 Mrs. Banks came across an old painting of the prophetess in the back parlour of a shop in North London. " The somewhat dingy walls were," she says, " to my great surprise, hung with fine old paintings in old frames, and seemed to

*Notes and Queries. 4th s., iv.. 213.
† Harrison's Mother Shipton Investigated, p. 62.
‖ Notes and Queries. 4th s., ii., 117.
‡ Notes and Queries, 4th s., ii., 235

me of great value. Amongst these my attention
was arrested by one larger than the others—an
ancient portrait of character so remarkable that
I could not refrain from asking whose it might be.
The answer was, ' Dame Shipton,' our ancestress,
commonly called Mother Shipton, and said by
some to be a witch.' There was nothing of the
conventional ' witch ' about the portrait, but there
was certainly an aspect of keen-eyed intelligence."
When Mrs. Banks, at a later period, wished to
examine the portrait again, the Shiptons had
removed, and all trace of them lost.

An engraving of Mother Shipton, in a chariot
drawn by a reindeer or stag, appeared in the
Wonderful Magazine, Vol. II., London, 1793.

In Kirby's *Wonderful Museum* (Vol. ii., p. 145)
there is a portrait of Mother Shipton, drawn by
Sir Wm. Ouseley from an oil painting in the
possession of Mr. Ralph Ouseley, of York, which
had been "present with the family of the pro-
prietor for more than a century." It represents a
melancholy-looking woman, with a broad-brimmed
hat, whose chin is being stroked by a monkey or
familiar.

In the *Gentleman's Magazine* for November, 1831
(Vol. ci., p. 401, 486), there is an engraving of an
ivory carving, which is conjectured to represent
the brazen head of Albertus Magnus, with Friar
Bacon, Dr. Faustus, and Mother Shipton. The
history of this curious carving is unknown, and
there may be doubt as to what it really is
intended to represent.

The weird creature represented on p. v. of this
volume is taken from the edition of the prophecies
issued in 1686. The following "portrait" is from
the same source.

MOTHER SHIPTON (from the prophecies of 1686).

Mr. Harrison is of opinion that the hooked nose, turned-up chin, and peaked cap of Mother Shipton, as shown in the picture on the edition of the prophecies issued in 1663 became gradually transformed into the figure of *Punch*, with which we are all so familiar. This theory he supports with much ingenuity in his little book, " Mother Shipton Investigated."

At a meeting of the Archæological Association, 27th May, 1863, Mr. J. O. Halliwell presented a woodcut of Mother Shipton from the 1662 edition. Mr. H. S. Cuming pointed out that the staff with the handle in the shape of a bird's head, was identical with the Egyptian *gom* or sceptre of augury used by the priests. He also made some observations on her "strange head-gear like a turban, with high cornuted crown, bending forward somewhat after the manner of the *corno ducale* of the Venetian doge and bonnet worn by Punchinello." He thought this was not the form with which she was generally represented. The high-peaked hat or *capatain* has become so much identified with Mother Shipton, "that it is looked upon almost as an attribute of the black art." The capatain was popular about the middle of the seventeenth century, but has, several times since then, come to the front in the whirligig of fashion.

Amongst the portraits of Mother Shipton we must not omit to name that which is borne on the wings of the *Euclidia Mi*,—a handsome moth, which is common in many parts of England, Scotland, and Ireland. Figures of it will be found in Newman, Wood, and Westwood, and other writers on Entomology. On the figure is what looks like the eye, hooked nose, and curved chin that has become traditionally associated with the name of the Yorkshire prophetess.

THE "MOTHER SHIPTON" MOTH.

I.

THE PROPHECIES

OF

MOTHER SHIPTON

In the raigne of King Henry the Eighth.

FORETELLING THE

DEATH OF CARDINAL WOLSEY, THE LORD PERCY, AND OTHERS,

As also what should happen in insuing time.

London, printed for Richard Lowndes, 1641.

The Prophecy of Mother Shipton, *in the Reign of King* Henry
the Eighth.

WHEN she heard King Henry the Eighth should
be King, and Cardinal Wolsey should be at York,
she said that Cardinal Wolsey should never come
to York with the King, and the Cardinal hearing,
being angry, sent the Duke of Suffolk, the Lord
Percy, and the Lord Darcy to her, who came
with their men, disguised, to the King's house,
near York, where, leaving their men, they went to
Master Besley to York, and desired him to go
with them to Mother Shipton's house, where
when they came they knocked at the door, she
said come in, Master Besley, and those honour-
able Lords with you, and Master Besley would
have put in the Lords before him, but she said,
come in, Master Besley, you know the way, but
they do not. This they thought strange that she
should know them, and never saw them ; then
they went into the house, where there was a great
fire, and she bade them welcome, calling them all
by their names, and sent for some cakes and ale,
and they drunk and were very merry. Mother
Shipton, said the Duke, if you knew what we
come about, you would not make us so welcome,
and she said the messenger should not be hanged.
Mother Shipton, said the Duke, you said the
Cardinal should never see York. Yea, said she,
I said he might see York, but never come at it.
But, said the Duke, when he comes to York thou
shalt be burned. We shall see that, said she,
and plucking her handkerchief off her head, she
threw it into the fire, and it would not burn ; then
she took her staff and turned it into the fire, and
it would not burn, then she took it and put it on
again. Now, said the Duke, what mean you by

this ? If this had burned (said she) I might have burned. Mother Shipton (quoth the Duke) what think you of me ? My love, said she, the time will come when you will be as low as I am, and that's a low one indeed. My Lord Percy said, what say you of me ? My Lord (said she) shoe your Horse in the quick, and you shall do well, but your body will be buried in York pavement, and your head shall be stolen from the bar and carried into France. Then, said the Lord Darcy, and what think you of me ? She said, you have made a great gun, shoot it off, for it will do you no good, you are going to war, you will pain many a man, but you will kill none, so they went away. Not long after the Cardinal came to Cawwood, and going to the top of the Tower, he asked where York was, and how far it was thither, and said that one had said he should never see York. Nay, said one, she said you might see York, but never come at it. He vowed to burn her when he came to York, and told him it was but eight miles thence ; he said that he will be soon here : but being sent for by the King, he died in the way to London at Leicester of a lask ; and Shipton's wife said to Master Besley, yonder is a fine stall built for the Cardinal in Minster, of Gold, Pearl, and King Henry, and he did so.

Master Besley seeing these things fall out as she had foretold, desired her to tell him some more of her prophesies. Master, said she, before that Owes Bridge and Trinity Church meet, they shall build on the day, and it shall fall in the night, until they get the highest stone of Trinity Church, to be the lowest stone of Owes Bridge ; then the day will come when the North shall rue it wondrous sore, but the South shall rue it for evermore ; when

Hares kindle on cold hearth stones, and lads shall marry ladies, and bring them home, then shall you have a year of pining hunger, and then a dearth without corn; a woeful day shall be seen in England, a King and Queen, the first coming of the King of Scots shall be at Holgate Town, but he shall not come through the bar, and when the King of the North shall be at London Bridge his tail shall be at Edenborough; after this shall water come over Owes Bridge, and a Windmill shall be set on a Tower, and an Elm tree shall lay at every man's door, at that time women shall wear great hats and great bands, and when there is a Lord Mayor at York let him beware of a stab; when two Knights shall fall out in the Castle yard, they shall never be kindly all their lives after; when all Colton Hagge hath born seven years Crops of corn, seven years after you heard news, there shall two judges go in and out at Mungate bar.

> *Then Wars shall begin in the Spring,*
> *Much woe to England it shall bring :*
> *Then shall the Ladies cry well-away,*
> *That ever we liv'd to see this day !*

Then best for them that have the least, and worst for them that have the most, you shall not know of the War over night, yet you shall have it in the morning, and when it comes it shall last three years, between Cadron and Aire shall be great warfare, when all the world is as a lost, it shall be called Christ's cross, when the battle begins, it shall be where Crookbackt Richard made his fray, they shall say, To warfare for your King for half-a-crown a day, but stir not (she will say) to warfare for your King, on pain on hanging, but stir not, for he that goes to complain, shall not

come back again. The time will come when
England shall tremble and quake for fear of a
dead man that shall be heard to speak, then will
the Dragon give the Bull a great snap, and when
the one is down they will go to London Town ;
then there will be a great battle between England
and Scotland, and they will be pacified for a time,
and when they come to Brammammore, they fight
and are again pacified for a time, then there will
be a great Battle at Knavesmore, and they will be
pacified for a while ; then there will be a great
battle between England and Scotland at Stokn-
more ; then will Ravens sit on the Cross and
drink as much blood of the Nobles as of the
Commons ; then woe is me, for *London* shall be
destroyed for ever after ; then there will come a
woman with one eye, and she shall tread in many
men's blood to the knee, and a man leaning on a
staff by her, and she shall say to him, What art
thou ? and he shall say, I am King of the *Scots*, and
she shall say, Go with me to my house, for there
are three Knights, and he will go with her, and
stay there three days and three nights, then will
England be lost, and they will cry twice a day
England is lost ; then there will be three Knights
in *Petergate* in *York*, and the one shall not know of
the other ; there shall be a child born in *Pomfret*
with three thumbs, and those three Knights will
give him three horses to hold, while they win
England, and all Noble blood shall be gone but
one, and they shall carry him to Sheriff *Nutton's*
Castle, six miles from *York*, and he shall die there,
and they shall choose there an Earl in the field,
and hanging their horses on a thorn, and rue the
time that ever they were born, to see so much
bloodshed ; then they will come to *York* to besiege

it, and they shall keep them out three days and three nights, and a penny loaf shall be within the bar at half-a-crown, and without the bar at a penny; and they will swear if they will not yield to blow up the Town walls. Then they will let them in, and they will hang up the Mayor, Sheriffs, and Aldermen, and they will go into Crouch Church, there will three Knights go in, and but one come out again, and he will cause Proclamation to be made, that any may take House, Tower, or Bower for twenty one years, and whilst the world endureth there shall never be warfare again, nor any more Kings or Queens, but the Kingdom shall be governed by three Lords, and then *York* shall be *London*; and after this shall be a white Harvest of corn gotten in by women.

Then shall be in the North, that one woman shall say unto another, mother, I have seen a man to-day, and for one man there shall be a thousand women; there shall be a man sitting upon St. *James* Church hill weeping his fill, and after that a ship come sailing up the Thames till it come against *London*, and the Master of the ship shall weep, and the Mariners shall ask him why he weepeth, being he hath made so good a voyage, and he shall say, Ah! what a goodly city this was, none in the world comparable to it, and now there is scarce left any house that can let us have drink for our money.

> *Unhappy he that lives to see these days,*
> *But happy are the dead Shipton's wife says.*

II.

THE

Strange & Wonderful History

OF

MOTHER SHIPTON,

Plainly setting forth

HER PRODIGIOUS BIRTH, LIFE, DEATH, AND BURIAL,

With an exact Collection of all her famous
Prophecys,
More compleat than ever yet before published;
and large explanations, shewing how they have
all along been fulfilled to this very year.

Licensed according to Order.
Printed for W. H. and sold by J. Conyers in Fetter-lane.
1686.

CHAPTER 1.

Of Mother Shiptons *strange Parentage, and the place of her birth.*

MOTHER SHIPTON (as all Histories agree) was a *Yorkshire* woman ; but the particular place is very much disputed, because several Towns have pretended to the honour of her Birth ; But the most credible and received opinion ascribes it to *Naseborough*, near the dropping well in the County aforesaid ; concerning her Pedigree or Parentage there are likewise very various reports ; Some say that her Father was a *Necromancer*, and that skill in the black Art thereby became intail'd upon her by inheritance ; but the common story (which therefore I shall follow, yet without forcing the Reader to believe it whether he will or no) is, That she never had any Father of humane Race, or mortal Wight, but was begot (as the great *Welch* Prophet *Merlin* was of old) by the Phantasm of *Appollo*, or some wanton Airial *Dæmon*, in manner following.

Her Mother (whom some Records call *Agatha*, and others *Emmatha*) being left an Orphan about the Age of sixteen, very poor, and much troubled with that grievous, but common disease, called by some idleness, and by others Sloth ; as she was once upon a time sitting, bemoning herself on a *shady* bank by the Highway side, this spirit appear'd to *her* in the shape of a very handsom young man, and smiling on her, *Pretty Maid* (quoth he) *why dost thou sit so sad ? Thou art not old enough to have thy Head pestered with the cares of the World ; prithee tell me the business, and doubt not but I will help thee out of all thy troubles.* The Maid (for

Maids there were in those days at her *age*) casting
up her eyes, and not suspecting a devil hid in so
comely a countenance, related to him her wants,
and that she knew not how to live ; *pish !* said he,
*that's nothing, be but ruled by me, and thou shalt never
lack ;* she hearing him promise so fairly, told him
she would ; and thereupon to draw her in by
degrees to destruction he first tempted her to Forni-
cation, and prevailed so far as to gain her, but his
Touches (as she afterwards confessed to the
Midwife) were as cold as Ice or Snow ; From this
time forward she was commonly once a day
visited by her Hellish Gallant, and never wanted
money, for still as she swept her house she should
find some odd pieces, as Ninepences, *Quarters* of
thirteen pence half-pennies, and the like, sufficient
to supply all her occasions.

CHAPTER 2.

*How Mother Shipton's Mother proved with child, how she fitted
the severe justice, and what hapned at Her delivery.*

THE neighbours observing *Agatha* without any
employ to live so handsomly, wondred exceedingly
how *she* came *by* it, but were more *surpriz'd* shortly
afterward, when they perceiv'd her to *be* with child,
which *she* could not long hide, for before her
delivery, she was as big as if she had gone with
half a dozen *children* at once ; whereupon she *was*
carried *before* a Justice, who chid and threatned
her for her Incontinency, but he was soon
silenced (for his Wife and all his Family being
present) *Agatha* said to him aloud, Mr. Justice,
Gravely you talk now, and yet the truth is, your
worship is not altogether free, for here stands two

of your Servant wenches, that are both at this time with child by you, pointing to them severally with her finger; at which both himself and the two Girls were so blank, That his wife plainly saw what she said was true, and therefore fell upon two poor Harlots like a fury, so all Mr. Justice and the Constable could do was not enough to keep the peace, and the whole Family was in such confusion, that *Agatha* for that time was dismist; and soon after was brought to bed in the Month of *July*, in the 4 year of the Reign of King *Henry* the 7th, which was in the year of our Lord 1488. Her travel was very grievous, and a most terrible clap of Thunder hapned just as she was delivered of this strange Birth, which afterward was so famous by the name of Mother *Shipton*. Nor could the Tempest affright the Women more than the prodigious Physiognomy of the Child; the Body was long, but very big-bon'd, great Gogling eyes, very sharp and fiery, a Nose of unproportionable length, having in it many crooks and turnings, adorned with great Pimples, which like vapors of brimstone *gave* such a lustre in the night, that her Nurse needed no other Candle to dress her by; and besides this uncouth shape, it was observ'd, that as soon as she was born, she fell a laughing and grinning after a jeering manner, and immediately the Tempest ceased.

CHAPTER 3.

By what Name Mother Shipton *was Christned, and how her Mother went into a Monastery.*

THE Child being thus brought into the *World*, under such *strange circumstances* was (though not

without some opposition) *ordered* at last by the
Abbot of *Beverly* to be christned, which was
performed by the *name* of *Ursula Soothtell;* For the
later was her Mothers, and consequently her
Maiden surname; and as for *Shipton*, it was the
name of her Husband, whom she afterwards
married, as will *appear* in the sequel of this History,
and in this *particular* most of the Authors I've
read have been foully mistaken; but to proceed,
when she was about two years old, her Mother
coming to be sensible of her evil, in holding a
correspondency with a wicked spirit, aplying
herself to several Religious men of great note in
those times, by whose grave Advice she grew
truly penitent, and (according to the fashion of
that Ages devotion) put her self into a neighbouring Monastery, having first put out her Child
with a piece of money to a Friend, and so spent
the Remainder of her days in the famous Convent
of the order of *St. Bridget*, neer *Nottingham*, in
prayers & tears, & other Acts of Pennance, to
expiate the wickedness of her youth; But
wonderful it is to relate the troubles that befel the
Nurse *she* was put to, for her father, the foul
Fiend, is reported several times to have visited
her, particularly one day the Nurse having been
abroad, when *she* returned she found her door
open, whereupon fearing she was robb'd, she
call'd three or four neighbors and their Wives to
go into the house with her, but before they got
well into the Entry, they heard a strange noise,
as if there had been a thousand Cats in consort,
which so dismaid them, that they all ran towards
the door endeavouring *to* get out agen, but *in* vain,
for every one of them had got Yokes on their
Necks, that they could not possibly return, but

soon after the Yokes fell off, and then a Coulstaff
was laid on 2 of the mens shoulders, upon which
an old Woman presented her self stark naked,
sometimes hanging by the heels, sometimes by
the toes, anon by the middle; with divers other
postures, while the women having all their Coats
turned over their ears, exposed their shame to
publique view, and so continued till a *Fryer*
accidently came to the house, and then they
were suddenly released ; but still the child having
been taken out of the cradle, could not be found,
till at last one of the company *looking* by chance
up the *chimny*, saw it stark naked sitting a straddle
upon the *Iron* to which the Pot-hooks was fastned,
whence they took it down without the least hurt,
and so far from being frighted, that it seemed by
its *monstrous* smiles to be very well pleased at these
pleasant Exploits.

CHAPTER 4.

Several other merry pranks plaid by Mother Shipton, *in Revenge
to such as abused her.*

As our *Ursula* grew up to riper years, she was
often affronted by reason of *her deformity*, but she
never fail'd to be revenged on those that did it ;
as one day all the cheif of the Parish being
together, at a *merry* meeting, she coming thither
occasionally on an Errand, some of them abused
her by calling her the Devils Bastard, and Hag-
face, and the like, whereupon she went away
grumbling, but so *ordered* affairs, that when they
was set down to Dinner, one of the principal
Yeomen, that thought himself spruce and fine,
had in an instant his *Ruff* (which in those days

they wore) pull'd off, and the Seat of an house of
Office clapt in its place; he that sate next him
bursting out into a laughter at the sight hereof, was
served little better, for his Hat was invisibly
convey'd away, and the Pan of a Close-stool
which stood in the next Room, put on instead
thereof. Besides this, a modest young Gentlewoman that sate at the Table at the same time,
looking at these two *worthy spectacles* of mirth,
endeavour'd all she could to Restrain laughing,
but could not, and withal continued breaking of
wind backward for above a quarter of an hour
together, like so many broad sides in a Sea-fight,
which made all the company laugh so extreamly,
that the Master of the house (being the chief Inn
in the town) was alarmed below therewith, and
desirous to share with his Guests in their mirth,
came running up Stairs as fast as his Legs would
carry him, but being about to enter the door, he
could not, and no wonder, since the oldest Man
living never saw a larger pair of horns than he had
on his head; But whilst they were gazing on one
another, as more than half distracted, they were
all reduc'd to the same condition they were in at
first, after which followed a noise, as if more than
a hundred persons were laughing together, but
nothing was seen.

CHAPTER V.

How Ursula *married a young man named* Toby Shipton, *and
strangely discovered a Theif.*

Our *Ursula* was now arrived at the four and
twentieth year of her Age, and though she was
none of the prettiest Maids in the Town, as you

may remember by her description, yet she long'd for an husband as much as the best of them, and at last obtained her desire. For whether she used any Love-powder or charms to enamour him, *or* whether the hopes of getting some money which she was *reported* to have, though nobody could tell how she should come by it, caused him to court her (as some men there are that would not only marry the Devils daughter, but his dam too for mony) I cannot certainly inform the Reader, but a Sweet-heart she had named *Toby Shipton*, by Trade a *Carpenter*, to whom she was shortly after *married*, and very comfortably they lived together, but never had any children.

It hapned about a Month after her *marriage* one of her Neighbours leaving her door carelesly open, lost a new Smock and Petticoat, stoln away while she was telling a Gossips tale of an hour long at next door, whither she went to fetch fire; which misfortune much troubling her, she made her mourn to our Mother *Shipton*, who did not go about like our little silly Conjurers with their Schemes and Figures to give a blind description of she *knew* not whom, but roundly told her such a Woman by name had stoln the things, adding, that she would make her *restore* them with a shame to her, and so indeed she did; For the next Market day before all the people this woman could not avoid putting on the smock over her other clothes, and the Petticoat in her hand, and so marched through the croud into the Market-cross, where the other was by *Mother Shipton's* directions to Receive them, dancing all the way and singing these words,

I stole my Neighbour's Smock and Coat,
I am a Theif, and here I show't.

And so when she came to the *owner*, pull'd off the Smock and gave *her Her* own with a Reverend courtesie, and so *departed*.

CHAPTER 6.

Her Prophecy against Cardinal Woolsey.

By these and several the like Exploits, Mother *Shipton* had got a name far and near for a cunning woman, or a woman of the forsight, so far that her words began to be counted Oracles, nor did she meddle only with *private persons*, but was advised with concerned *people* of the greatest quality; among which *number* at that time was Cardinal *Woolsey*, when it was *reported*, that he intended to live at *York*, she publickly said, *He should never come thither*, which coming to his ear, and being much offended, he caused three Lords to go to her, who came disguised to *Ring-house* near *York*, where leaving their men, they took a Guide and came to Mother *Shipton's*, where knocking at her door, she cryed out within, *Come in Mr.* Beasly (their Guide) *and those noble Lords with you*. Which much surprized them that she should know them, for when they came in, she called each of them by their name and treated them with Ale and Cakes, whereupon said one of the Lords, *If you knew our Errand, you would not make so much of us, you said the Cardinal should never see* York. *No*, said she, *I said he might see* York, *but never come at it; Well*, saies the Lord, *When he does come thou shalt be burnt*. Then taking off her Linen Kercheif from her head, saies she, *If this burn, then I may burn*, and immediately flung it into the fire before them, but it would not burn, so that after it had lain in the flames a quarter of an *hour*, she took it out again not so much as singed, Hereupon one of the Lords askt her what she thought of him, *My Lord*, said she, *the time is coming when your Grace will be as low as I am, and that is a low one indeed.* Which proved true, for shortly after he was beheaded.

Nor was her speech of the *Cardinal* less verified, for he coming to *Cawood*, went to the top of the Tower, and askt where *York* was, which being shewn him, he inquired how far it was thither, *For* (qd. he) *there Was a Witch said, I should never see* York. Nay says one present, *your Eminence is mis-inform'd, she said you should see it, but not come at it.* Then he vow'd to burn her when he came there, which was but eight Miles distant, but behold, immediately he was sent for back by the King, and dyed of a violent looseness at *Leicester*.

CHAPTER 7.

Some other Prophecies of Mother Shipton's *relating to these times.*

At divers other times, when Persons of Quality came to visit her, she delivered the several Prophecies following, that is to say

1 Prophecy.

Before Owse-bridge *and* Trinity-Church *meet they shall build in the day, and it shall fall in the night, until they get the highest stone of* Trinity-Church *the lowest stone of* Owse-bridge.

Explanation.

This came to pass: for *Trinity Steeple* in *York* was blown down with a Tempest, and *Owse-bridge* broken with a Flood, and what they did in the day-time in repairing the Bridge, fell down in the night, till at last they laid the highest Stone of the Steeple for the Foundation of the Bridge.

2 Prophecy.

The North shall Rue it wondrous sore,
But the South shall Rue it for evermore.

3 Prophecy.

You shall have a year of Pining Hunger, & shall not know of the War over-night, yet shall you have it in the Morning, and when it happens, it shall last three years, then will come a woman with one Eye, and she shall tread in many mens blood up to the knee.

4 Prophecy.

Then may a man take House or Bower, Land or Tower for one and twenty years: but afterwards shal be a white Harvest of Corn gotten in by Women, Then shall it be, that one Woman shall say to another, Mother! I have seen a man to day.

5 Prophecy.

A time shall happen, when a Ship shall come sailing up the Thames, *till it come against* London, *and the Master of the Ship shall weep, and the Mariners of the Ship shall ask him,* Why he weeps, since he has made so good a Voyage? *And he shall say,* Ah! what a goodly City this was, none in the World comparable to it, and now there is scarce left an house, that can let us have drink for our Money.

Explanation.

These last words were sadly verified after the dreadful Fire of *London,* 1666, when there was not an House left all along *Thames*-side, from the *Tower* to the *Temple;* As for the words *before,* they being darkly delivered, are not like to be understood, till time, that both discovers and absconds all things, shall bring the matters signified to light.

CHAPTER 8.

Her Prophæcies in Verse to the Abbot of Beverly.

THE Abbot of *Beverly* giving her a Visit one day, told her, *That as he had found several things that she had formerly said to be exactly true, so he was perswaded she was not Ignorant in those which for the future were to Ensue, and therefore requested her to impart some of her fore-Knowledge to him, for which Favour (tho' more than his deserts could command, yet) shall he neither want a tongue to acknowledge nor a heart to endeavour a Requital for so great an Obligation.* Mr. Abbot, says she, *leave of complementing, I am an old Woman who will neither flatter nor be flatter'd by any, yet shall answer your Desires as far as I may.* And thereupon did in mystick verses discover to him the greatest Accidents that have happen'd in *England*, from that day to this, as in the following explanations will appear.

Prophecy.

When the Cow doth ride the Bull,
Then the Priest beware thy Skull.

Explanation.

By the Cow was meant *H*. 8. who gave the Cow in his Arms as Earl of *Richmond*, & the Bull betoken'd Madam *Ann* of *Bulloigne*, not only as the first syllable of her name, but because her Father gave the black Bulls Head in his Crest, and when the King *married her* immediately after hapned the dissolution of Monasteries, and *restraints* laid on the Priests.

Prophecy.

For a sweet pious Prince make Room,
And in each Kirk prepare a Broom.

Explanation.

This is meant of King *Edward* the sixth, in whose time the

Protestant Religion was established, and the Popish Superstitions swept out of the Kirk, an old word used still in *Scotland* for the Church.

Prophecy.

Alecto *next assumes the Crown,*
And streams of blood shall Smithfield *drown.*

Explanation.

These lines decipher Q. *Mary.* called *Alecto* (a name of one of the Furies) for her cruelty to the Protestants, of whom great numbers were then burnt in *Smithfield.*

Prophecy.

A Maiden Queen full many a year
Shall Englands *War-like Scepter bear.*

Explanation.

Spoken of Q. *Elizabeth,* who Reigned extreamly beloved by her Subjects, and dreaded by her Enemies above fourty years.

Prophecy.

The Western Monarchs Wooden Horses
Shall be destroyed by the Drakes *Forces.*

Explanation.

The King of *Spains* mighty Navy in 88, destroyed by the *English* Fleet under Captain DRAKE.

Prophecy.

The Northern Lyon over Tweed,
The Maiden Queen shall next succeed,
And joyn in one two mighty States,
Then shall Janus *shut his Gates.*

Explanation.

This relates to King *James,* who having been many years King of *Scotland,* the Crown of *Englana* by Queen *Elizabeths*

Death fell to him, whereupon he came over *Tweed* to take up his Residence here, and so joyned the two Kingdoms under one Government; And as for *Janus* shutting his Gates, you must know *Janus* was one of the Heathen gods, that had a Temple at *Rome*, the Gates of which were never shut but in times of Peace, alluding to which our Prophetess *here* declares the peaceful Reign of King *James*.

Prophecy.

Forth from the North shall mischief blow,
And English Hob *shall add thereto ;*
Mars *shall rage as he were wood,*
And Earth shall drunken *be with blood*.

Explanation.

This relates to our late Lamentable Civil Wars.

Prophecy.

But tell's what's next, Oh cruel fate !
A King made Martyr at his gate.

Meaning the Execrable *murther* of that most excellent Prince *Charles* the First.

The just King dead, the Woolfe shall then
With Blood usurp the Lyons Den.
But death shall hurry him away,
Confusion shall a while bear sway,
Till fate to England *shall restore*
A King to Reign as heretofore ;
Who mercy and justice likewise
Shall in his Empire exercise.

These Prophecies we have seen fulfilled by *Cromwells* Usurpations, The Committee of Safetys Confusions, and our Gracious Soveraigns Miraculous Restauration.

Prophecy.

Triumphant death rides London *through,*
And men on tops of Houses go.

21

Explanation.

The first Line points out the great Sickness in *London*, 1665. And the second, the dreadful Fire the Year following.

> *Let this suffice, the night comes on,*
> *You must depart, and I be gone,*
> Apollo *does forbid my Rhimes,*
> *For to unvail succeeding times.*

Having said this, Mother *Shipton* arose, and the admiring Abbot (who took all these Prophecies you must conceive, in writing) giving her many Thanks, *returned* home.

CHAPTER 9.

Of Mother Shiptons *Death, Burial, and Epitaph.*

THIS famous Prophetess continued several years esteemed, as the *Sybil* or *Oracle* of these times. At last being threescore and thirteen years of Age, she found the time in the black Book of Destiny approaching, wherein she must give a final Adieu to this World, which she fore-told to a day to divers people, and at the hour *predicted*, having taken solemn leave of *her Friends*, laid her self down on her Bed and dyed, on whom a Poet of that Age bestowed this

EPITAPH.

> *Here lies She who never Ly'd,*
> *Whose* Skill *so often hath been try'd;*
> *Her Prophecies shall still survive,*
> *And ever Keep her Name alive.*

FINIS.

III.

THE LIFE and DEATH

OF

MOTHER SHIPTON,

Being not only a true Account of her strange Birth; the most important Passages of her Life; but also all her Prophesies, now newly Collected, and Historically Explained, from the time of her Birth, in the Reign of King *Henry* the Seventh, until this present Year 1667. Containing the most important Passages of State during the Reign of these Kings and Queens of *England* following,

Viz.
{ *Henry* the Eighth. } { King *James*.
{ *Edward* the Sixth. } { King *Charles* the First.
{ Queen *Mary*. } { King *Charles* the Second.
{ Queen *Elizabeth*. }

Strangely preserved amongst other writings belonging to an old *Monastry* in *York-shire*, and now Published for the Information of Posterity.

Licens'd and Entred according to Order.

LONDON,

Printed for Benj. Harris, at the Stationers' Arms and Anchor under the Piazza of the Royal Exchange, 1684.

Beloved Countrey-men,

THE great Fame, and general received Opinion of *Mother Shipton*, with the Credit she hath obtained by those several *Prophesies* uttered by her, which since in the greatest measure have come to pass: These Considerations (I say) put me upon a Resolution to search out by my best endeavour, the Parents, Place, and Time wherein this *Mother Shipton* Flourished. Many old Manuscripts and rusty Records I turned over, but all in vain; at last I was informed by a Gentleman (whose Ancestors by the Gift of King *Henry* the Eighth, enjoyed a *Monastary* in those parts) that he had in his keeping some ancient Writings which would in that point satisfie my desire, were they not so injured by Time, as now not legible to Read; however, I not despairing to find out their meaning, with much Importunity desired to have a sight of them; which having obtained, I took of the best Galls I could get, beat them grosly, and laid them to steep one day in good white-Wine, that done, I distilled them with the Wine; and with the distilled Water that came off them, I wetted handsomly the old Letters, whereby they seemed as fresh and fair, as if they had been but newly written; here did I find her Life and Prophesies copied out by an imparcial hand, which I have in this book presented to thy view, together with an Exposition upon her Prophesies, for the better understanding of them, and which may serve to them whose leisure will not permit to read, or want of money forbid to buy more Voluminous Authors; this (I say) may serve to them instead of a Chronicle, wherein they may find related the chiefest matters performed in each King and Queens Reign since the time wherein she flourished: much more might be added, but lest I should exceed the bounds of an Epistle, and like the Citizens of *Mindium*, make my Gates too bigg for my City, I shall here break off abruptly, wishing thee as much pleasure in the Reading thereof, as I had in the Writing of it; and so

Farwel,

R. Head.

POSTSCRIPT.

Courteous Reader, let me desire thee Candidly to pass over some seemingly Impossibilities in the first sheet, (allowing the Author Licentia Poetica *in her description) and some Actions performed in her Minority; and only to weigh the more serious part of her Prophesies, wherein (if thou bee'st rational) I doubt not but thou wilt receive ample satisfaction.*

THE CONTENTS.

LIFE OF MOTHER SHIPTON

CHAPTER I.

What her Father and Mother were, and what wonderful things happened at her Birth, as also the place of Her Nativity.

IN the Second Year of King *Henry* the Seventh, which was the Year of our Lord One thousand four hundred eighty and six; there lived a Woman called *Agatha Shipton*, at a place called *Naseborough* near the *Dropping-Well*, in *York-shire*. She came of poor Parentage, who died and left her to shift for her self, at the age of fifteen. After their decease, she still inhabited in the old House; but being now deprived of those helps she formerly enjoyed conducible to a lively-hood, she was constrained to seek relief from the Parish; which she did, but with so much regret and grief, that she seemed in her begging rather to command Almes, than in an humble manner to desire it. At length she arrived to that pass, that she was upon the matter starving, rather than she would be beholding to the charity of any.

The Devil looking on her poverty to be great, and knowing her evil inclinations by her complexion (for you must understand, that the Devil is a good Scholar, well read in all things, and much acquainted with the constitutions of all sorts of persons.) I say, perceiving that she was willing to accept of any proposition to change her condition: He one time as she was sitting Melancholy under a Tree by a River side,

accosted her in the form of a very handsome
young man, well apparel'd with all things suitable
to a youthful garb, Pretty Maid (quoth he),
Why dost thou sit so sad? Thy age is too slender
for thy head to be troubled with cares of the
World; come tell me what is the matter, and if it
lie within my power to assist thee (as I am sure it
doth) thou shalt not want a friend of me.

Agatha casting up her eyes, and there seeing a
face so lovely, could not suspect a Devil hid in
that comely shape; whereupon in a lamentable
tone she exprest all that troubled her, informing
him of her great wants, and that not knowing how
to work, she could not provide what her necessities
required: Pish (said the Devil) this is nothing, be
ruled by me, and all shall be well; she told him
she would; hereupon he ordered her to meet
him at the same place the next day, and he would
bring some friends along with him, for he told her
he resolved to marry her; she promised him she
would, and accordingly they met. He came riding
upon a stately Horse, with a pillion behind him
for his Spouse, attended by a great many Gallants
(as they appeared) well mounted, and in a noble
equipage.

His Divel-ships attendants soon conveyed his
Mistriss behind him, as she imagined; not in the
least doubting the reality of all she saw.

They needed neither switch nor spur to hasten
them forward, the Jades were fiery enough of
themselves, and ran with that swiftness that the
wind could not over-take them in their full speed;
soon they arrived at their journies end, where
seemed to be a very stately House, with a great
pair of Gates, which at their approach opened by
a Porter with his stick, in his Livery-gown:

Alighting, she went in, where she saw a great many servants, which seemed, at the sight of her and their Master, to show much respect and obeisance.

Now did the Devil command rich Garments to be brought, which she was immediately cloathed with and being thus richly attired, she was ushered into a great Hall, where was a long Table furnished with all the varieties the whole world could afford ; at the upper end of which table she was placed, next her the Friend her intended husband ; all the rest of the guests did place themselves as they thought fit. As they had the choicest cheere, so had they the best of Wines, and sweetest Musick.

Dinner being ended, they fell to Dancing ; and now could my lecherous Divil stay no longer, but he must needs walk a corant with his Mistris into another private room, and there courted her to lust ; the simple Girl consented, and so they both went to bed together, with the Ceremonies of Marriage. His touches (as she confessed to the Midwife that delivered her of her Devilish Offspring) were as cold as ice or snow. After they had lain a little while together, he told her what he was, and what she must do hereafter, if she intended to live happy and delightful dayes. First, he told her that he was no Mortal, but a Spirit, immaterial, and not burdened by a body, nor hindred by any material thing ; So that I can when I please pierce through the Earth and ransack its Treasures, and bring what precious things I please from thence to bestow on those that serve me. I know all rare Arts and Sciences, and can teach them to whom I please. I can disturb the Element, stir up Thunders and Lightnings, destroy the best of things which were created for the use of man ; and can appear in what shape, or form I please. It will be too long to describe my power, or tell thee what I can do ; but will only tell thee what thou shalt do. That being done, I will give thee power to raise Haile, Tempests, with lightning and Thunder ; the Winds shall be at thy command, and shall bear thee whither thou art willing to go, though never so far off ; and shall bring thee back again when thou hast a mind to return. The hidden Treasures of the Earth shall be at thy dispose and pleasure, and nothing shall be wanting to compleat thy happiness here. Thou shalt moreover, heal or kill whom thou pleasest ; destroy or preserve either man or beast ; know what is past, and assuredly tell what is to come. Here note by the way, the Devil is a Lyar from the beginning, and will promise more by ten millions, than he knows he is capable to perform, to the intent he may insnare and damn a soul.

This poor ignorant wretch easily believed what this Grand Deceiver of Man-kind told her ; and being ravish't with the thoughts of being so highly preferred ; she condescended to all the Devil would have her do : Whereupon he bid her say after him, in this manner : *Razielellimibammirammis hziragiaPfonthonphanchiaRaphaelelhaverunatapinotambec azmitzphecat jarid cuman hapheah Gabriel Heydon turris dungeonis philonomostarkes sophecord bankim*. After she had repeated these words after him, he pluckt her by the Groin, and there immediately grew a kind of Tet, which he instantly suckt, telling her that must be his constant Custom with her morning and evening ; now did he bid her say after him again, *KametzadtuphOdelPharaz TumbaginGallFlemmngrnVictowDenmarkeonto*, having finisht his last hellish speech, which the chiefest of his Minions understand not, out of which none but the Devil himself can pick out the meaning; I say, it thundered so horridly, that every clap seemed as if the vaulted roof of Heaven had crackt and was tumbling down on her head; and withal that stately Palace which she thought she had been in, vanisht in a trice : so did her sumptuous apparel : and now her eyes being opened, she found herself in a dark dolesom Wood; a place which from the Creation had scarce ever injoyed the benefit of one single Sun-beam. Whilst she was thinking what course to steere in order to her return, two flaming fiery Dragons appear'd before her tied to a Chariot, and as she was consulting with herself what was best to be done, she insensibly was hoisted into it, and with speed unimaginable conveyed through the Air to her own poor Cottage.

CHAPTER II.

How the Devil constantly visited her, in what Forms and Shapes; what strange things she did to those that offended her, harming some, and making sport with others; and at length brought to bed of a Child, which is now commonly called Mother Shipton.

BEING come home, the Neighbours flockt about her, having mist her two or three daies, shrewdly suspecting some mischief had befallen her; but when they beheld her face, they were all amased to see such a strange alteration in her countenance, in so short a time; and here the Proverb was verified in her : *She lookt as if a Hagg had rid her*. Before she met with this wanton Devil, she lookt plump and fresh, which were all the good qualities she had in her ill featured face; but now that red plumpness vanisht, and there was nothing to be seen but a pale shriveled skin on her cheek, which for want of flesh seemed to fall in her mouth, to be devoured by her hunger-starved jaws. Those about her which were charitable minded, pitied her, comforted and gave her moneys, which with a great deale of disdain and scorn she threw them saying, she wanted not, nor stood in need of their Almes; for look ye here (said she), is money enough, plucking her hand out of her pocket, the people drawing near her, discovered that what was in her hands, was nothing else but some *Aspin-leafs;* and notwithstanding, they endeavoured to perswade her that she was mistaken in supposing that to be money, yet she would not believe them; so strong a Power the Devil had gotten over her already.

In fine, she bid them all be gone, for now she began to take little delight in humane Society: It was not long that they had left her, before the Devil (with whom she made an Hellish Contract,) came in to see her, in the same handsome young form as he first appeared unto her, telling her that he came to supply the company of those she had so wisely dismist, that she needed not the society of any humane creature, for he would not fail to be constantly with her; always bringing with him what should not onely serve for a bare Livelihood, but her Delight, Pleasure, and Satisfaction: Hereupon by the Devil's command, there instantly appeared seemingly, a compleat noise of Musick, with Dishes of Meat, great variety of the choicest and most pleasing sort; which so ravisht *Agatha*, that she fell to the ground in a profound and deep trance. One of her Neighbours coming in this while, wondered to see *Agatha* lying on the floor motionless; however out of pity and commiseration, she kneeled down, and having crossed

herself, and said a short prayer, she endeavoured
to waken *Agatha*, but using what means she could,
it all signified nothing ; she shook and pincht her,
and pulled her by the nose, yet still she lay insensibly:
This Neighbouring woman being strangely amazed
and scared hereat, ran out amongst the rest of the
Neighbours, crying out that poor *Agatha Shipton*
was suddenly struck dead, and so desired them to
go into the house with her, and they should there
be the eye-witnesses of the truth thereof ; whereupon several went and found what this woman had
said to be seemingly true ; but one wiser than the
rest, stooped down, and perceiving that she
breathed, spake aloud, Friends ye are all mistaken,
Agatha is not dead, but in a trance, or else she is
bewitched ; she had scarce uttered these words
before *Agatha* began to stir, and soon after raised
herself on her leggs, crying out in a very distracted
tone, What make ye here, vile wretches ? Cannot
I enjoy my pleasures, but ye must be Eves-drop-
ping ; get ye gone, as having nothing to do here ;
and hereupon she fell a dauncing, which they
wondered at because they could hear no Musick.
At length, *Agatha* turning about, and seeing they
were not gone ; said, if ye are resolved thus to
disturb me, and will not go, I will make ye : this
something affrighted them, for they now verily
believed she was a witch ; and as they were has-
tening away with all imaginable speed, a sudden
strong wind hoisted them a great height into the
air, falling all to the ground again without the
least harm, onely some shame to the women, for
they descended with their heads downwards, and
their coats over their ears, their lower parts appearing all naked to the astonished spectators:
the men were seen like over-grown Goats with

large horns on their heads, and women riding on their backs : which sights as they produced inexpressible wonder, so amidst their amazement, they could not but burst out into excessive laughter.

This wonderful and unexpected exploit, was instantly noised all about the Countrey, which occasioned a great resort of people to the place where *Agatha* lived ; which so perplext her by their undesired visits, that she resolved within herself to be revenged on some of them ; which by the Devil's help she effected ; mischieving some in their persons, others in their cattel, and others in their credits ; one had a Horse that dyed suddenly and being opened, there was found in his stomack fish-hooks, and hair, instead of hay and oats. Another going to sit down at Table with persons of good quality at dinner-time, and thinking himself very spruce and fine, had in an instant his Ruffe pull'd off, and the Seat of an House of Office clapt on in its place, he that sate next him, breaking out into great laughter at the sight thereof, was served little better ; for his Hatt was invisibly conveyed away, and the Pan of a Close-stool which stood in the next room, put on instead thereof ; A modest young Gentlewoman which did sit at the Table at that time, and was come on no other errand but to see this young witch which was so much talked of ; looking on these two worthy spectacles of laughter, endeavoured all she could to refrain laughing, but could not, and withall continued farting for above a quarter of an hour ; this made them all laugh so extreamly, that the Master of the House was alarum'd (below) therewith, and being desirous to share with his Guests in their mirth, came running up stairs as fast as his leggs would carry him, about to enter the door, he could not, and no wonder, since the oldest man living, never saw a larger pair of horns than he had on his head : Whilst they were gazing one on another as more then half distracted, they were all reduced to the same condition they were in before ; after which there followed a noise, as if an hundred persons were laughing together, but nothing at all was seen.

These persons fearing something worse might befall them if they staid any longer, made all the haste they could to be gone: *Agatha* knowing their intent, resolved to take her farwel of them by serving them one trick more, which was thus : As they were about to mount on Horseback, they were pelted with rotten apples, dung, and stuff that smelt worse than can be imagined. As they rid through the Town, such men as thought they rid singly, were all observed to have behind them each man a deformed old woman; and as their faces differ'd all one from another, so did their habits, which were all tatter'd and ragged, and patcht with a hundred colours ; fear, shame, and the hooting of the people, made them put spurs to their Horses, neither did they forbear the switch, nor anything that might add speed to their Horses heels ; so that it may be said, they rather flew than rode ; how could it be otherwise ? *for needs must he go whom the Devil drives*.

Coming home, they declare what wonderful things they had seen performed, though by a young one, yet as they believed, the greatest witch in the world : this news being so generally spred, came at length to the ears of the Justices, who now thought it high time to question and bring into examination a person that was so much

talked of, and might, if let alone, do a great deal
of mischief.

CHAPTER III.

*How Agatha Shipton was apprehended and brought before a
Justice ; what her Confession was, her Mittimus being made
to be sent to Prison : how she escaped by the help of her friend,
the Fiend ; she is retaken, and being found with Child, is
bail'd.*

Agatha is now no longer suspected, but plainly
known to be a witch, doing something or other
daily which was very remarkable ; she hath been
frequently observed to walk alone muttering to
herself, and having been watcht by some, they
have seen her stamp upon the ground thrice, then
wound her hands over her head, lastly, she spake
one word thrice, and in the twinkling of an eye,
the skie hath been dark and gloomy, though clear
before, which belcht out nothing for half an hour
but flames, thundering after a most hideous
manner.

But now the time draws on, wherein she must
give an accompt for what she hath done, and in
order thereunto, she is apprehended by two resolute fellows, who were not a whit daunted when
they entered the house, though Toads, Adders,
and such like noisome creatures crawled up and
down the house, but could not chuse but be much
startled when they had seiz'd her and were carrying
her, to hear such a terrible crack of thunder, the
house at that time reeling to and fro like a Cradle.

However they carried her before the Justice,
where being brought, she was strictly examined
by him ; she not a jot daunted, told him that she
had more authority than he, and that notwith-

standing his power, she could command one that could over-rule him when he list; That she was a Princess, and could have at her beck a thousand Spirits of the Air, and as many of the Earth and Water; That she could raise a Tempest presently that should overturn his house about his ears; and that you may know, it lyes not in your power to detain me, three words shall procure my liberty: hereupon she said *Vpdraxi*, call *Stygicon Helluox*, she had no scarce uttered the last word, before there came in a horrid winged-Dragon, which immediately took her up, and carried her away from the amazed Justice and Attendants about him, half dead with fear.

This so affrighted all that heard of it, that none would undertake to meddle with her more; so that she had a considerable time of respite. But she now began to be more admired than before, being discovered by the great swelling of her Belly, to be with Child: The people could not tell what to think, or who should be the Father, concluding that none would be so vile and wicked as to have Copulation with a Devil incarnate; neither could they believe a Spirit had either desire or power, to generate with any humane Creature; while people were generally passing their verdicts on *Agatha*, she was once more taken and brought before a Justice, and amongst other questions, was asked, whether she was with Child, she acknowledged it; nay father, that it was begot by no mortal Wight: The Justice gave no credit to what she said, as looking on her as an ignorant seduced Woman; and so askt her what Bail she could produce, intending to deferr the business till she was delivered; in this very nick of time two Gentlemen as they appeared by their habits, voluntarily proffered themselves, which as soon as accepted for Baile, vanisht presently, however *Agatha* had permission to go home.

CHAPTER IV.

What kind of shape Mother Shipton *had when she was born
How she was put to Nurse at the charge of the Parish; and
what strange things were seen in that House where she was
Nurst, during the term of four years.*

THE usual time of forty weeks being expired, her Mother after many strange and horrible torments which she underwent in her Travel, was at last delivered (by the rare skill and industry of her Midwife, and others of that Sex) of her which is now called, *Mother Shipton,* which proved the conclusion of her miserable life. But her entry into the World was such a tertor to all that beheld her, that several credible persons then present, have several times confest, that they never beheld the like: Such strange and horrible noises, that the persons concern'd about her, could scarce find so much courage in themselves as to continue in the place where she was; much less when they beheld the strange and unparallel'd Physiognomy of the Child, which was so misshapen, that it is altogether impossible to express it fully in words, or the most ingenious to Limn her in colours, though many persons of eminent qualifications in that Art have often attempted it, but without success; therefore according to the best observations of her, take this true, though not full account of her features and body: she was of an indifferent height, but very morose and big bon'd, her head very long, with very great goggling, but sharp and fiery eyes, her nose of an incredible and unproportionable length, having in it many crooks and turnings, adorned with many strange Pimples of divers colours, as red, blew, and mixt, which like Vapours of Brimston gave such a lustre to her affrighted spectators in the dead time of the Night, that one of them confest several times in my hearing, that her Nurse needed no other light to assist her in the performance of her duty : Her Cheeks were of a black swarthy Complexion, much like a mixture of the Black and yellow juandies ; wrinkled, shrivelled and very hollow, insomuch, that as the Ribs of her Body, so the impression of her teeth were easily to be discerned, through both sides of her face, answering one side to the other, like the notches in a Valley, excepting only two of them which stood quite out of her mouth, in imitation of the Tushes of a wild Bore, or the Tooth of an Elephant, a thing so strange in an Infant that no age can parallel : Her Chin was of the same complexion as her Face, turning up towards her mouth, and shreeks being heard, from an unknown cause, as if there had been a more than ordinary correspondence between her Teeth and it.

Her Neck so strangely distorted, that her right shoulder was forced to be a supporter to her head, it being propt up by the help of her Chin, in such sort that the right side of her body stood much lower than her left ; like the reeling of a Ship that failes with a side winde. Again, her left side was quite turned the contrary way, as if her body had been sctew'd together piece after piece ; and not rightly placed : her left shoulder hanging just Perpendicular to her Fundament.

Her Leggs very crooked and misshapen : The Toes of her feet looking towards her left side ; so

that it was very hard for any person (could she
have stood up) to guess which road she intended
to stear her course ; because she never could look
that way she resolved to go.

After she had remained under the care of her
Nurse, for the space of a Moon ; or thereabouts,
her Mother being unable to provide for her, she
was put out to Nurse at the charge of the Parish,
to a Poor Woman hard by in the Town where she
continued for the space of half a year or thereabouts, the house not being any waies disturbed
at all, till at last, her Nurse having been abroad
amongst some of the chief of the Parishioners,
either to procure something of their Charity for
her subsistence, and the maintenance of her Family
or else to fetch her money from the Overseers of
the Poor, for Nursing the Child ; and returning
home to her House, she found her dores unbard
and wide open, whereat she much amazed and
affrighted, ran to her next Neighbour, and
acquainted her that she was quite undone, for her
house was broken open and robbed ; the man immediately riseth from his Dinner, carrying his
bread and Chese in his hand, accompanied with
his Wife and another labouring man ; approaching
the door, endeavoured to enter, but before they
could all get quite in, there was immediately a very
strange noise heard in the next Room to them, as
if it had been a consort of Catts, which so affrighted them, that they all ran towards the door
endeavouring to get out again, but it was in vain ;
for at their approach there were great long yoaks
about their Necks, in the form of a Cross, or turned
stile ; so that they could not possibly return ; and
while they were thus striving and crying out for
help ; their yoaks at last fell off, and a coule-staff,

or Brewers-sling laid upon the mens shoulders ; upon which an old woman presented herself naked, sometimes hanging by the Heels, sometimes by the Toes, and anon by the Middle ; with divers other postures, they continuing for the space of near half an houre, in such sort, that the poor men were never more tired in clearing of Leggs, nor less pleased at any thing than in being constrained to humour this piece of hellish activity.

After they had got a discharge from this their new employment, the house being now quiet, and they a little recovered their sences, and missing the women, they ran further into the house, where at last they found them lying flat upon their bellies, their clothes being turned backwards over their heads, two great black Catts were playing *Hocus-Pocus* upon their posters, which the men in vain attempted to drive away, until at last their own slavery procured the womens freedom from that employment, though they changed not much for the better, for as they were coming out of that Room, in the next there stood a pair of Yarwingles, made in the form of a Cross, upon which the women used to put great skains of Yarn, that so they may wind it of with more ease and less trouble : These being placed in the middle of the Room, the two men and two women were forced to take the four ends thereof in their hands, and so daunce round about the Room one after the other, until such time as they were almost tired to death, carrying upon every one of their shoulders an Imp in the likeness of a Monkey or Ape, which hung close upon them ; and when ever they slackened their pace, these Sprits pricked them forward, continuing this recreation for a very considerable time; and being cloy'd with this kind of diversion, they vanished quite out of sight, leaving these poor wretches as weary, as astonished; who (notwithstanding) no sooner perceived themselves at liberty but they presently quitted the house, and soon after addressed themselves to several of the Neighbourhood, aquainting them with what had happened, which caused great amazement amongst them, and immediately the whole Town was in an uproar; and the Minister and several of the most eminent Inhabitants, consulted together what the occasion thereof should be, and what to do in the business, some of them threatning the informers; others thinking they were distracted: But at last they resolved to go to the House; yet when they came near, there arose a great dispute amongst them who should first enter, which at last was agreed upon; and the Parson (with his Congregation attending him in the rear;) gave them the first onset, and entering the door quivering and shaking, they heard the Nurse-child cry in a most hideous and dolefull manner; whereupon there was suddenly a noise like the treading of people upon stones, though the house in any place had no other than an earthen floor; at which the Child ceased, and a very sweet musical harmony of several notes was heard, and all presently vanished again: after which the Minister and Inhabitants entring, and searching the House, at length missing the Child, one of them looking up the Chimney, saw the Cradle wonderfully hanging about three yards high without any support: which being as strangely conveyed down again; they encouraged the Nurse, and leaving her in the House (though affrighted) they departed for the present.

CHAPTER V.

How Mother Shipton *whilst but very young at Nurse, was daily Visited by Spirits. in divers Shapes and Formes; and what Pranks they play'd during her abode there.*

MOTHER SHIPTON now grew apace, and as her stature encreased, so did her deformity: Her supposed Father (the foul fiend) omitted not a day wherein he visited not the House where she was sometimes visibly in the form of a Cat, Dog, or Hog; at other times invisibly by noises, so terrible, as it so affrighted the Nurse, that she oftentimes resolved to deliver up her charge, and forsake her habitation; sometimes she came in a pleasant humour, either singing or playing on an Instrument, which was usually a Scotch Bag-pipe.

Her Nurse sometimes was in great perplexity, not knowing what was become of her, for an whole day together; but when she was in her greatest search after her, she saw her oftentimes drop through the Roof of the House: Going out, upon her return, she many times found her Child stretcht out to a prodigious length, taller than the tallest living, and at other times as much decreased or shortned. The poor woman's work for the major part, was only to rectifie what these Spirits disordered about her House; the Chairs and Stools would frequently march upstairs and down, and they usually plaid below at Bowles with the Trenchers and dishes: Going to dinner, the meat was removed before she could touch a bit of it, which things as they much troubled the Nurse, so they gave much satisfaction to *Mother Shipton*, as it appeared by her Monstrous smiles: Now and then to pacifie her Nurse, when she saw her much vext, hereat, she would say, be contented, be contented, there is nothing here will harm you.

To be short, the Nurse was so continually ter-
rified by these apparitions, that she resolved to
complain to the Parish; and having made known
the truth of what had past, in commiseration to the woman almost distracted, they removed
Mother Shipton to another place, where she was put
to School, being of an age now fitting for it.

CHAPTER VI.

How Mother Shipton *was put to School, learning more in a day
than other Children could in a Month: how she was jeered by
her School-fellows for having such a monstrous long Nose: and
what pranks she plaid upon them, by way of Revenge: growing
now very famous.*

MOTHER SHIPTON was now grown a lusty Girl;
and as she was left to the care of the Parish, so
the Parish took care that she should have the common sort of Learning; that is to say, Reading and
Writing bestowed upon her. Comming to School
her Mistris began to instruct her, as other Children,
beginning with the Cris-cross-row as they call'd it,
showing and naming onely three or four Letters at
first, but to the amazement and astonishment of
her Mistris; she exactly pronounced every Letter
in the Alphabet without teaching. Hereupon her
Mistris, shewed her a Primmer, which she read as
wel at first sight, as any in the School, and so proceeded in any Book was shown her.

As this produced wonder in her School Mistris,
so hatred and envy in her Comrades; some flouted
her for her monstrous long Nose, others endeavoured to beat her, and all strove to mischief her,
but she valued them not, revenging herself upon
every one of them, that intended her harm. Some

were Pinch't, and yet no hand seen that did it; others struck speechless when they were about to say their Lessons, not being able to utter a word; and none escaped from being served one scurvy trick or other. This so enraged the Parents of these Children, looking on *Mother Shipton* the sole cause hereof; that she was discharged the School, and so left to the wide World.

She hath been often seen when alone, to laugh heartily; at other times to talk by her self, uttering very strange riddles, which occasioned some of the more sober sort to converse with her, receiving such strange things from her, as required a long study to find out the meaning.

Never a day passed, wherein she related not something very remarkable, and required the most serious consideration. And now it was that people flockt to her far and near (her fame was so great), to be resolved of their Doubts, all returning wonderfully satisfied in the Resoluution of their questions.

CHAPTER VII.

How several persons came to Mother Shipton, *for her Predictions; and how a rich Heire being deceived by her Maid, fell sick of Grief, and dyed.*

AND now *Mother Shipton* begining to grow Famous in the World, for her notable Judgment in things to come: There resorted to her House a number of people, of all sorts, both old and young, rich and poor; Especially, of the female Sex, *viz.* Young Maids and Wenches, who have alwaies a great Itching desire, to know when they shall be Married; as also, what manner of Husbands they

shall have; to which she gave such satisfactory
answers, both for the Persons, and time; that no
sooner could a young Maid get into the Teens,
but she would presently trott to *Mother Shiptons*,
to be resolved of her doubt. Now though she
were not Mercenary herself, but refused great
Gifts, when proffered unto her; yet did she keep
a young Wench, who rather than fail, if they
forgot to open their purse to her, she would
remember to open her mouth to them, and tell
them, that her Dame *Shipton*, nor she, could not
be maintained with thanks, but that the belly
required meat to feed it; and that it was money
which made the Mare to go. One day their came
a certain young Heir thither, whose Father was
sick, to be resolved by her, whether he should live
or die; but *Mother Shipton* could by no means be
wrought upon to tell him any thing; whereupon
he proffered the Maid great store of Money, if she
could by any means perswade her Dame, to fulfil
his request; the Wench greedy of Money,
promised him fair; and that if he would come the
next Morning, he should be certain to be resolved;
in the mean time, she importuned her Dame with
the most cunning Rhetorick that she could invent;
but she was deaf to all entreaties, and would by
no means be induced thereto, whereupon the
Wench resolved with her self, rather than to lose
the money, to give him an answer of her own
intention; which the next morning she performed
in these words.

The Grave provided hath a Room,
Prepare for Death, thy Hour is Come.

The young Gentleman having received this
answer, went home very joyfully, hopeing presently

to reap the Golden Crop which his Father had
sown, and to be in an instant possessed of all his
vast estate; but the sequel proved quite contrary;
for by that time he came home, great hopes of
amendment appeared in his Father, who each day
grew better and better, so that in a short time he
became perfectly well. This unexpected recovery
of the old man, struck such a dump in our
young Heir, that he presently took his Bed, fell
extream sick, and in a short time grew so extraordinary ill, that all the symptoms of a dying man
appeared in him : The old man, who had carked
and cared all his life time for his Son, (having no
more Children but he) was very desirous of his
life, and to know whether he should recover;
whereupon he sent to *Mother Shipton* about the
same ; who knowing by her Art, what her Maid
had done, sufficiently did chide her for the same ;
threatning upon such another offence, to turn
her out of her service. In the mean time, the
Messenger was come to her House, who having
delivered his errant, was returned back with this
answer.

> *For others Deaths who do gape out,*
> *Their own unlook't for, comes about :*
> *Earth he did seek, ere long shall have,*
> *Of Earth his fill, within his Grave.*

The old man having received this answer, was
much troubled, as thinking his own Death predicted thereby, not imagining in the least, what
his Son had done; but he was soon quit of that
suspition, for within two daies the young man
dyed; when by a Servant (who knew the passages)
he was informed the truth of the whole matter.

CHAPTER VIII.

Mother Shipton's Prophecies concerning *King Henry* the Eighth's *journey into* France ; *of Cardinal* Wolsey, *and other things.*

ABOUT this time, some differences arising betwixt *King Henry* the *Eighth*, and the *French King;* great preparations of War were made in *England*, the Drums beating in every County, to summon Voluntary Valour to express it self, in defence of their King and Country. Many Heroick Spirits, who made Honour their Aime, not dreading any dangers for the attaining thereof, now listed themselves *Bellona's* followers: so many appearing under *Mars* his Banner, that he who was furnished with Limbs, and an Estate, to decline the Service was adjudged a Coward. There was then living in the North, a young Heir, who was newly come to his Estate, one whose Tongue was all fire, and his heart all ire, who would kill Thousands with words, but durst not adventure to do any thing in deeds. This Gallant being by some of his equals, pricked on to make his appearance in the field of *Mars*, and not to lie sleeping at home, when Fame summoned him forth to Action, he knew not what to doe in this case; loath was he to lose his loved Life, and yet the aspersion of a Coward, though to a Coward himself, is of all things most odious: He therefore promised them fair; that none should be more willing than he, to spend his blood in the quarrel of that Country, from whence he received his dearest life; but yet resolved with himself, not to set one step forward in that path of danger, till he had first consulted with *Mother Shipton*, concerning what success he should have in his journey; if bad, he was resolved by a feigned sickness to evade, thinking it no policy of a man to part away with that life in an instant, which with great cost and care, had been many years in bringing up.

Hereupon he hasts to our Northern Prophetess, acquaints her with his Condition, and very earnestly desires of her (as she to whom nothing was unhid) that she would unfold to him whether good, or bad fortune should be his attendant, in this his Expedition. *Mother Shipton* though she perceived his sheepless courage to be every way unanswerable to that of a Soldier, yet foreknowing what should come to pass, returned him this answer; which without more ado, fully satisfied him to proceed, and perform what he had promised; the answer was this.

When the English Lyon *shall set his paw on the* Gallique *shore then shall the* Lillies *begin to droop for fear: There shall be much weeping and wailing amongst the Ladies of that Country; because the* Princely Eagle *shall join with the* Lyon, *to tread down all that shall oppose them: and though many* Sagitaries *shall appear in defence of the* Lillies, *yet shall they not prevaile; because the dull Animal of the* North *shall put them to Confusion; and though it be against his will, yet shall cause great shame unto them. Now shall the* Mitred Peacock *first begin to* plume, *whose* Train *shall make a great show in the World, for a time; but shall afterwards vanish away, and his great* Honour *come to nothing; which shall take its end at* Kingston.

The Explanation of the Prophecy.

By the *English Lyon* was meant the King of *England*; and by setting his *Paw* on the *Gallique shore*, the Landing of his Army in *France*, which not long after he did; by the *Lillies beginning to droop with fear*, was signified the great trouble and perplexity of the *French*, the *Lillies* being the Armes of *France*; the *weeping and wailing amongst the Ladies of that Country*, denotes the miseries and destructions incident to War, the Sword, Famine, Destruction and Desolation being inseparable Companions; by the *Princely Eagle joyning with the Lyon, and treading down all that should oppose them*, is meant *Maximilian* the *German Emperor* (whose Armes were the *Eagle*) who not only joyned in Amity with King *Henry*, but also took wages of him, and served him in his Wars as an hired Soldier; by the *Sagitaries that appeared in defence of the Lillies*, was meant the *French* Cavalry, the chief strength of *France*, consisting of Horse-men. who appeared like *Sagitaries*, that is to say, half Men, and half Horses, gave *Mother Shipton* to use that expression; and whereas it is said, *yet they should not prevail* it fell out so accordingly; for notwithstanding, all the oppositions of the *French* Armies, King *Henry* proceeded on vigorously, conquering and taking several towes of importance. as *Tourney*, *Bulloign*, &c. But to come to that which most nearly concerns the matter, *viz.* the success of our young Heir, in this expedition. which was hinted forth unto him in these words, *because the dull Animal of the North, shall put them to Confusion; and though it be against his will, yet shall cause great shame unto them;* by the *dull Animal of the North*, was meant this freshwater Soldier, who according to the Prophesie, put the *Frenchmen* to confusion, and great shame; for passing the Seas with King *Henry*, being mounted on a stately Horse as both Armies confronted each other, he being in the Head of the Battel. just before the Charge, some body striking his Horse, the Jade carried him perforce upon the Enemy, with such violence, as put their front into some disorder, which being perceived by our men, they presently so seconded him, that in fine, the *French* very fairely ran away, leaving the *English* a glorious victory, purchased with a little cost.

By this means was *Mother Shiptons* Prediction fulfilled to the disgrace of the *French*, and great praise of the young Gallant; for the rest of the Prophesie, the Interpretation thereof runs thus.

By the *Mytred Peacock* was intended *Cardinal Wolsey*, signified by that Bird, because of his great Pride, who being but a poor Butchers son of *Ipswich* in *Suffolk*, grew to such height, that he thought himself Superior to the chief Nobles of the Land, living in such splendor as not to be Parallel'd, according to the Prophesie; *Whose Train shall make a great show in the World;* and whereas it is said, *the Peacock should then begin to plume*, so it was, that when King *Henry* had taken the City of *Tourney* in *France*, he made *Wolsey* Bishop thereof, who soon after rose to the highest degree of Honour a Subject could be capable of, which afterwards (as the Prophesie says) *vanished away, and his great Honour came to nothing:* And lastly, whereas it is said, he should *have his end at Kingston ;* the Cardinal being told of this Prophecy, would never pass through the Town of *Kingston*, though lying directly in the Road, from his own House to the Court ; but afterwards being arrested of High Treason, by the Earl of *Northumberland* and Sir *Anthony Kingston* the Lieutenant of the Tower sent unto him, his very name (remembring this Prophesie) struck such terror to his heart, that he soon after expired.

CHAPTER IX.

Her Prophesie to the Abbot of Beverly, *concerning the downfall of* Abbeys, Nunneries, Priories, &c., *with other things.*

MOTHER SHIPTONS Predictions coming thus effectually to pass, spread her Fame far wider than it was ; insomuch, that many who looked upon her as a crackt-brain'd Woman, now began to admire her, and to esteem of her words as Oracles. And as the nature of *English* people is, rather to desire to know what is to come, than to seek to rectifie ought what is done amiss; so the greatest part of her visitants, came only to be resolved, of what she knew, would come to pass, of which number was the Abbot of *Beverly*, who fearing the downfall of religious Houses, and a change of the Religion then professed, putting on the counterfeit Clothes of a Lay-person, he came to *Mother Shiptons*, and knocking at the dore, she being within, called to him, and said, Come in, Mr. *Abbot*, for you are not so much disguised, but the Fox may be seen, through the Sheeps skin ; it is not those Clothes makes you a Lay-person, no more than a Long-Gown makes a man a Lawyer; come, take a stool and sit down, for you shall not goe away unsatisfied of what you desire, and thereupon she began to utter forth her Prophecies in this sort.

> When the Cow doth ride the Bull,
> Then Priest beware thy Scull,
> And when the lower Shrubs do fall,
> The great Trees quickly follow shall.
> The Miter'd Peacocks lofty Pride,
> Shall to his Master be a Guide,
> And one great Court to Pass shall bring,
> What was neer done by any King.
> The Poor shall Grieve, to see that Day,
> And who did Feast, must Fast and Pray.
> Fate so Decreed their Overthrow,
> Riches brought Pride, and Pride brought Woe.

These Prophecies were thus Explained: by the *Cow* was meant King *Henry*, who gave the same, by reason of the *Earldom of Richmond*, which was his Inheritance: and the *Bull* betokeneth Mrs. *Anne Bulloign*, whom the King took to Wife, in the room of *Queen Catherine*, her Father gave the Black *Bulls* head in his Cognizance, and was his Beast; and when the King had married *Queen Anne*, then was fulfilled the second line of the Prophesie, *viz., then Priest beware thy Scull*, for what a number of Priests, Religious and Secular, lost their heads, for offending of those Laws made to bring this matter to pass.

> And when the Lower Shrubs do fall,
> The great Trees quickly follow shall.
> The Miter'd Peacocks lofty Pride,
> Shall to his Master be a Guide.

Cardinal Wolsey (who is here intended by the *Miter'd Peacock*) in the height of his Pride, and vastness of his undertakings to erect two fair Colledges, one at *Ipswich* where he was born, the other at *Oxford* where he was bred; and finding himself unable to endow them at his own Charges; he obtained License of *Pope Clement* the Seventh, *Anno* 1525, to suppress forty small

Monasteries in *England*, and to Lay their old Lands to his *new Foundations*, which was done accordingly; and the poor people that lived in them, turned out of doors; many of the Clergy were very much against this action of *Wolseys.* especially, *John Fisher*, Bishop of *Rochester*, alleging for the same an *Apologue* out of *Æsop*, that *the Iron Head of the Axe, craved a handle of the Wood of Oaks, only to cut off the seere boughs of the Tree; but when it was a compleat instrumental Axe, it felled down all the Wood;* applying it *That the suppressing of those smaller Houses, would in fine, prove Destructive to all the rest;* which came to pass accordingly; for King *Henry* seeing the Cardinals power to extend so far, as to suppress these *lower Shrubs*, he thought his Prerogative might stretch so far as to fell down the *Great Trees;* and soon after dissolved the *Priory of Christs Church* nigh *Aldgate* in *London,* now known by the Name of *Dukes-place*, and which was the richest in Lands, and Ornaments, of all the *Priories* in *London,* or *Middlesex;* and which was a forerunner of the Dissolution of all the rest; and which not long after came to pass.

> *And one great Court to pass shall bring,*
> *What was ne'er done by any King.*

By the *Great Court*, is meant the Parliament, the Supreamest Court of *England*, who in the Twenty seventh of King *Henry's* Reign, *Anno* 1539. *To support the Kings States, aud supply his wants, Conferred on the Crown, all Religious Houses, which were not able clearly to expend above Two hundred pouuds a year;* the great ones not long after following the same fortune of the smaller, which was ne'er done (though attempted) by any King before.

> *The Poor shall grieve to see that Day.*

The *Abbots* and *Priors* being most bountiful House-keepers, relieving all comers and goers, got themselves much reputation for their Hospitality.

> *And who did Feast, must Fast and Pray.*

By the Dissolution of these Houses, many thousands were driven to seek their fortunes in the wide World, and become utterly exposed to want, when *Monkish* profession was without possession; many a young *Nun* proved an old Beggar, and were forced to fast for want of Victuals, who formerly had it provided for them, to their hands.

Fate so Decreed their overthrow,
Riches brought Pride, and Pride brought woe.

The great Riches and Pride of the *Monks* and *Fryars* was (no doubt) the main cause of their overthrow ; for whatsoever was the pretence, questionless profit was the Rope which pulled these Religious Houses down.

All these things coming to pass before such time as this *Abbot* died, caused him to have a great esteem of *Mother Shipton*, and to value her Prophecies more than ordinary conjectures; though at first, he could not tell what to make of her Ambiguous Lines, which, like the *Oracles*, formerly delivered at *Delphos ;* rather brought one into a Labyrinth of confused conjectures, then satisfied the expectation, until by the Clue of Time, the Riddles were manifest, and that which at first seemed so hard, now appeared to the understanding, as easie : However, he at present kindly thanked *Mother Shipton*, and liberally rewarded her Maid (who else would have put him in mind of his neglect), much admiring that she should be so clear-sighted, as to see through his counterfeit Dress; resolving afterwards to be more informed by her, concerning future events; he at that time took his solemn leave of her, and returned home.

CHAPTER X.

Her Prophecies concerning King Edward *the Sixth : the Rebellion of the Commons : The Death of the Duke of Somerset with other things.*

Not long had the *Abbot* been at home, but his *Abby* was visited by some instruments employed by the Lord *Cromwel* for that purpose. He who knew what was intended by this Complement, thought it not safe to strive against the Stream, and therefore quietly surrendered his *Monastary*, into the Kings hands. And he perceiving *Mother Shiptons* Prophecy plainly fulfilled, in the downfall of those Houses, which were judged Impregnable against all the assaults of Malice and time; Considering the strange Revolutions of so short a space: he was very desirous to be more fully informed of the future. In this Resolution he repairs again to *Mother Skiptons*, whom he now accosts more familiarly, than he did before, making himself plainly known unto her; telling her that as what she had formerly spoken, he had found to be true in the event; so his Judgment persuaded him, she was not ignorant of those things which were for the future to ensue; and therefore desired her, she would not be nice in imparting of this her fore-knowledge unto him; for which so great favour, though it were more than his deserts could Command, yet should there never in him be wanting a grateful tongue to acknowledge, and a grateful heart to be thankful unto her, for so great a favour.

Mr. Abbot (said she) leave off Complementing, as more fit for Courtiers, and Lovers, and not agreeable to an old Woman, who will neither flatter, nor be flattered by any: and for what you came about, I shall not be squeamish to fulfil your request, let me therefore desire you, to lend me your attention; and thereupon (after some short pause) she thus began.

> *A Prince that never shall be Born,*
> *Shall make the Shaved Heads forlorn.*

> *Then shall Commons rise in Armes,*
> *And Womens Malice cause much harmes.*
> *O deadly Pride !   O hateful Strife !*
> *Brothers to seek each others Life.*
> *Ambition shall so deadly spread,*
> *The* Griffin *fierce shall lose his Head.*
> *Soon after shall the* Lyon *die,*
> *And mildness usher Cruelty.*

These ten lines being Prophecies of the Actions in King *Edwards* Reign ; for the Readers benefit ; (before we proceed any further in her Predictions), we will unfold the meaning of them by themselves, that we may not too much burthen their memory ; but by variety add a pleasure to the reading of them.

> *A Prince that never shall be born,*
> *Shall make the Shaved Heads forlorn.*

By the Prince *that never shall be born*, is meant King *Edward* the Sixth, of whom all reports do constantly run, that he was not by Natural Passage delivered into the World, but that his Mother's Body was opened for his Birth, and that she died of the Incision the fourth day following ; and by the *Shaved Heads*, is understood the *Monks, Fryars*, &c., who are said to be become *forlorn :* the Reformation beginning, with the beginning of King *Edwards Reign :* and the *Popes Priests* put down, as his Supremacy was before.

> *Then shall Commons rise in Armes.*

King Edward having set out certain Injunctions, for the Reformation of Religion as the Commissioners passed to divers places for the establishing of them, many scorns were cast upon them, and the farther they went from *London*, as the people were more uncivil, so did they more rise into insolencie and contempt ; for in *Cornwel*, the Commons flocked together, having killed one of the Commissioners, and albeit Justice was done upon the offenders, the principle of them being Executed in several places, yet could not their boldness be beaten down with that severity, but that the mischief spread farther, in *Wilt-shire*, and *Somerset-shire*, where the people supposing that a *Common-Wealth* could not stand without Commons, beat down Inclosures, and laid Parks, and Fields, Champion. The like Commotions followed in *Sussex, Hamp-shire, Kent, Gloucester-shire, Warwick-shire, Essex, Hartford-shire. Leicester-shire, Worcester-shire,* and *Rutland-shire,* but the greatest of all, was in *Devon-shire* and *Norfolk :* the one Headed by *Henry Arundel* Esquire, Governour of the *Mount* in *Cornwel,* the other by *Robert Ket* a *Tanner* of *Windham* in *Norfolk :* Those of *Devon-shire,* were accounted above ten thousand, who with a close and smart Siege, Surrounded the City of *Exeter,* which they brought to extream misery, having a potent Foe abroad, and famine sorely raging within ; insomuch, as they were fain to bake Bran and meal moulded up in Clothes, for otherwise it would not stick together; at last the Rebels were routed from thence, by the Lord *Privy Seal,* with the loss of a Thousand of their Number, and soon after totally routed, at a place called *Clift-heath.* Those of *Norfolk,* were judged to be more dangerous ; both because their strength was great, being estimated to be above Twenty Thousand ; as also the City of *Norwich* was a friend unto them, or at least wished them no harm : This rude rout Encamped on *Monshold-hill,* a place impregnable in some sort, being near to *Norwich ;* against whom was sent the Marquis of *Northampton,* and afterwards the Earl of *Warwick,* who made many Sallies upon the *Rebels,* with various success ; had the Rebels kept in this Fort, they might have tired out the Earl, His horse being useless against them ; but they relying on an old Prophesie, came down into *Dussin-dale* and quitted the Fort.

CHAPTER XI.

Her Prophesies concerning the Death of the Lady Jane Grey. *the burning of the Martyrs. of* Wyats Rebellion. *the Death of Queen* Mary, *and Cardinal* Pool.

A vertuous Lady then shall die,
For being raised up too high.

The Lady *Jane Grey,* who out of dutifulness to her parents, assuming the Title of Queen upon her, for her offence, lost her head : This Lady *Jane* was a woman of most rare and incomparable perfections ; for besides her excellent beauty, adorned with all variety of vertues, as a clear sky with Starrs, as a princely Diadem with Jewels ; she was the mirror of her time, for her Religion and Education in the Knowledge of the Liberal

Sciences, and skill in Languages, for in Theology, in Phylosophy, in all the Liberal Arts in the Latine and Greek Tongues, and in the Vulgar Languages of divers near Nations, she far exceeded all of her Sex, and every one of her years.

> *Her Death shall cause anothers joy,*
> *Who will the Kingdom much annoy.*

The Death of the Lady *Jane* was supposed to be a rejoicing to *Queen Mary*, and who by restoring Popery, and the Persecutions that the professors of the Gospel suffered in her time, is said to bring the Kingdom to annoy.

> *Miters shall rise, Miters come down,*
> *And streams of Blood shall Smithfield drown.*

By the Miters are meant the *Bishops*, who in the Change of Religion found great Change; very few of them keeping their Seats, wherein they had been seated by King *Edward* the sixth the names of the *Bishops* thus put down, were these, *Cranmer Arch-Bishop* of *Canterbury*, *Ridley Bishop* of *London*, *Poynet Bishop* of *Winchester*, *Holgate Arch-Bishop* of *York*, *Bush Bishop* of *Bristol*, *Bird Bishop* of *Chester*, *Hooper Bishop* of *Worcester* and *Glocester*, *Barlo Bishop* of *Bath* and *Wells*, *Scory Bishop* of *Chichester*, *Ferrar Bishop* of *St. Davids*, *Coverdale Bishop* of *Exeter*, *Taylor Bishop* of *Lincoln*, and *Harley Bishop of Hereford*; in the room of these *Bishops* thus put down, several *Bishops* were raised, as Cardinal *Pool* made Arch-bishop of *Canterbury*, *Bonner Bishop* of *London*, *Gardiner Bishop* of *Winchester*, *Heath* Arch-bishop of *York*, *Holeman Bishop* of *Bristol*, *Cotes Bishop* of *Chester*, *Brook Bishop* of *Glocester*, *Pates Bishop* of *Worcester*, *Bourn Bishop* of *Bath* and *Wells*, *Christopherson Bishop* of *Chichester*, *Morgan Bishop* of *St Davids*, *Tuberville Bishop* of *Exeter*, *White Bishop* of *Lincoln*, and *Parfew Bishop* of *Hereford*.

And streams of Blood shall Smithfield *drown*.

Great was the number of *Martyrs* burned in *Smithfield* in this Queens Reign, under the Bloody hands of *Bonner Bishop* of *London*, and Dr. *Story*, Dean of *St. Pauls*; the first persecuting by wholesale, the second by retaile; the names of all those who in this place thus testified their faith, by the loss of their Lives, would be too long here to recite: the chief of them were, Mr. *John Rogers*, Mr. *John Bradford*, Mr. *Robert Glover*, &c

England shall join in League with Spain,
Which some to hinder strive in vain.

Queen *Mary* intending to match her self with *Philip* King of
Spain, the bruit thereof being spread amongst the people, was
by them ill resented, as dreading to be under the yoak of a
stranger; to hinder the same (amongst others) Sir *Thomas Wyat,*
a *Kentish Knight,* took Armes, with a great party assisting him.
The Queen hearing of his Commotion, sent a Herald to him to
desist, which he refusing to do. she resolves upon force, sending
the Duke of *Norfolk* with five hundred *Londoners* against him:
but these Soldiers bearing more affection to *Wyats* cause than
the Queens. forsook their Leader, and their Loyalty together,
and joyned themselves with *Wyats* Faction; who much elated
with this supply, presently resolves for *London,* promising to
himself easie entrance into that City, and hearty entertainment
therein; but contrary to his expectation, coming to *Southwark,*
he found all the Towers of the *Tower,* and the tops of the square
Steeples neer the Bridg foot on the other side, planted with
Ordnance against him. so that both Church and State threatened
his ruine; so that seeing no good to be done there. with a swift
March (having the Darkness of the Night for his Coverture) he
hasteth to *Kingston,* passed the River, and comes to *Knights-*
Bridg, before almost any had notice of his Motion.

Here he divides his Army into two parts, Five hundred of
them wheels down towards *White-Hall,* but could not force their
passage into it; Himself with the rest of the Army went directly
to *Charing-Cross,* where he met with some opposition, but
nothing daunted thereat, he marched directly down the *Strand*
and *Fleet-street,* and coming to *Ludgate* promised himself entrance
into the *City,* but finding the Gate close-shut, and well fortified
against him, with Men and Ammunition, his hopes then began
to fail him; retreating to *Temple-Bar,* he was faced with some
Horse, where after a short Fight, he submitted himself Prisoner,
being first carried to *White-Hall* to be examined, from thence to
the *Tower* and soon after to the Scaffold, where he received the
rewards of his Rebellion.

The Lyoness *from life retires,*
And Pontificial Priest Expires.

By the *Lyoness* is meant Queen *Mary,* who having Reigned
five years and some odd months, dyed of a Dropsie, though others
say of Grief for the absence of her Husband, King *Philip,* and

others again, for *Calice* (taken not long before) and that she should say, if after she was dead they ripped her up, *they would find* Calice *written on her heart.*

The Pontifical Priest signified Cardinal *Pool*, who expired within a few hours after the Death of *Queen Mary.* This Prelate was of Princely extraction, his Mother *Margaret* being Daughter to George Duke of *Clarence;* when he was a young man, he was brought up together with Queen *Mary*, and being a zealous Catholick during King *Edwards* Reign, suffered a voluntary exile for the same; when the marriage with Prince *Philip* and Queen *Mary* was made up, he returned into *England,* was made Arch-bishop of *Canterbury.* more moderate than some other of his fellow *Bishops*, having a favourable inclination towards the Protestants: he survived the Queen but few hours, and was buried in his own Cathedral at *Canterbury*, with this short and modest Epitaph on his plain Monument *D E P O-SITUM CARDINALIS POLI.*

CHAPTER XII.

Her Prophesies concerning the Reign of Queen Elizabeth ; *the change of Religion ; the attempts of the Papists. upon the Queen; the* Spanish *Invasion ; the burning of* Pauls *steeple; the death of the Queen of* Scots ; *the reducing of* Ireland ; *the beheading the Earl of* Essex, &c.

The Lyon *fierce being dead and gone,*
A Maiden Queen shall Reign anon.
Those who sighed, then shall sing,
And the Bells shall Changes Ring.
The Papal power shall bear no sway,
Romes trash shall hence be swept away,
The Locusts sent from the seven Hills.
The English Rose shall seek to kill.
The Western Monarchs Wooden Horses,
Shall be destroyed by the Drakes forces.
Troy novant's *Triumphant Spire,*
Shall be consum'd with flames of Fire.

More wonders yet! a Widowed Queen,
In England *shall be headless seen.*
The Harp shall give a better sound,
An Earl without a Head be found.
Soon after shall the English Rose,
Unto a Male her place dispose.

These lines being a Prophesie of the most re-markable Actions during the Reign of Queen *Elizabeth*, are to be interpreted after this manner.

The Lyon *fierce being dead and gone,*
A Maiden Queen shall Reign anon.

Queen *Mary* is here meant by the *fierce Lyon;* so called, not so much for the Cruelty done by *her*, as by the *Bishops* and *Priests* was done under *her;* for take her in her self, secluded from bloody Councillors, and she was a most Merciful, Pious, Just Prince; but in respect of the Blood that was shed, and the Persecutions then suffered, she is here termed a fierce *Lyon*: After whom is said, *A Maiden Queen to Reign anon*, meant by Queen *Elizabeth*, one who was the Mirrour of her Sex and Age, who for above forty years, to the admiration of envy it self, managed the affairs of this Kingdom; having when she began, few friends that durst help, and leaving no Foes when she died that could hurt her; acting her part so well whilst here she Reigned that History can scarcely afford us one Prince to be matched to her Fame, in all considerable particulars.

Those who sighed then shall sing,
And the Bells shall changes Ring.

Many who sat and sighed in the daies of Queen *Mary*, by reason of the hot persecution, being forced to forsake their Houses, because they would not forsake their Religion; now that Queen *Elizabeth* began to Reign, their mourning was turned into joy, their sighing into singing; returning from their exile, with Psalms of thanksgiving in their mouths: where their *Bells* rang such *Changes* in Religion, that the Mass was put down, and the Common Prayer set up: Popery banished, and reformation established; the Ministers of the Gospel advanced, and the Shaveling Priests, Monks and Fryers, depressed.

The Papal Power shall bear no sway ;
Romes *trash shall hence be swept away.*

Soon after the Queens coming to the Crown, a Parliament began at Westminster, wherein the Laws of King *Henry* the eighth against the See of *Rome* were renewed, and those of King *Edward* the sixth, in favour of the Protestants revived, and the Laws by Queen *Mary* made against them repealed : Uniformity of Prayer and Administration ot Sacraments was enacted with a Restitution of first Fruits and Tenths to the Crown; and the Queen acknowledged to be the *only and Supream Governour* of her Kingdomes : The People in each place beating down Superstitious *Pictures and Images,* which blind and misguided zeal had set up.

The Locusts sent from the seven hills,
The English Rose *shall seek to kill.*

By the Locusts are meant the Priests, Fryers, and Jesuits, who spread all the world over in greater numbers than the Locusts did in the Land of *Egypt ;* and by the seven Hills is meant *Rome,* which is built upon seven Hills ; and by the *English Rose* is signified Queen *Elizabeth,* whom the Priests and Jesuits by their Instruments did often attempt to kill ; so that if we seriously consider her Reign, we shall scarcely find any Prince, whose life was so often attempted as hers, of which to give you some Examples would not be impertinent to our purpose, and first in her Sisters Reign ; *Stephen Gardiner* Bishop of *Winchester,* and other *Romanists,* offended with her Religion, so wrought with Queen *Mary,* suggesting that she was consenting to *Wyats* insurrection, that she was sent prisoner to the Tower, and (as it is said) a Warrant intended to be sealed for her Execution, had not King *Philip* interceded. After she came to the Crown she was as incident to troubles as the month *April* is to showers. *Spain, France* and *Scotland* combining against her, *Pope Pius Quintus* by his Bull deposes her, in prosecution whereof, the Earles of *Northumberland* and *Westmoreland* rise up in Rebellion, being to have been assisted by the Duke *D'alva* out of the Low-Countries, but out of these troubles she was delivered by their Confusion. After these *Leonard Dakers,* second son to *William* Lord *Dakers* of *Gellesland,* endeavoured to bring her into trouble, being intrusted by her with competent forces, which he intended to have imployed to her detriment failed in his hopes and Power; and brought both shame and ruine to himself. Next did *Thomas* and *Edward Stanley* younger sons to the Earl of *Darby*, with several others, plot against her; all which ended in their Ruine and her safety. These failing, Captain *Stuckley* promised to perform wonders against her, but his mountaines proved not so much as mole-hills, he being slain in *Barberry*, his design failed. But to speak of personal attempts against her, one *Somervile* drew his Sword in the Court to have slain her: Doctor *Parry* a *Spaniolized Italian* intended to have Pistoled her as she walked in her privy Garden: *Savage, Windsor, Salisbury, Tilney*, and others, conspired to kill her, the which they waited several times to effect: one *William Stafford* by the instigation of the *French* Ambassador, undertook to kill her: Doctor *Loper* one of her sworn Physicians, for a summ of money, engaged to Poyson her: and to conclude all, one *Edward Squire*, formerly belonging to her Stable, with a mortifferous confection, Poysoned the Pomel of her Saddle, when she was riding out; from all which notwithstanding, though she were maliciously poysoned, she was miraculously preserved, and died in peace, *March* 24, 1603; maugre all the malice of her enemies.

The Western Monarchs *Wooden Horses,*
Shall be destroyed by the Drakes *Forces.*

By the Western *Monarchs* Wooden Horses, is meant the King of *Spains* great Armado, in the year 1588, by them termed Invincible, though the success of it answered not the name, being by Sir. *Francis Drake* and others, brave sons of *Neptune* and soldiers of *Mars*, met withal, fought with, and really vanquisht, most of it sunk, and the rest destitute and scatter'd, being chased by our Ships past the 57 degree of *Northern Latitude*, and there left to be pursued by hunger and cold; a victory so remarkable, that time, nor age, will ever wear the remembrance thereof away.

Troy novant's *Triumphant spire,*
Shall be consum'd with Flames of Fire.

By *Troy novant* is meant *London*, which in ancient writings is called *Troy novant;* and the Triumphant Spire, signifies *Pauls-steeple*, which in the year 1561, the fourth of *June*, strangely fell on fire, burning for the space of five full hours, in which time it melted all the Lead off the Church, only the Stone Arches escaping the fury thereof; sundry causes were attributed by sundry persons, of this fire; some that it was casually blasted with Lightning; others that it was mischievously done by Art,

Magick ; and others (which was most likely done) by the neg-
ligence of a Plummer carelessly leaving his coales therein. The
Queen was much grieved for this mischance, but by her bounty,
the Cities liberality, and a Contribution from the Clergy, it was
afterwards repaired, only the blunt Tower had not the top thereof
sharpened into a spire as before.

> *More wonders yet ! a widowed Queen,*
> *In* England *shall be headless seen.*

The Widowed Queen signifies the Queen of *Scots*, the Mother
of King *James*, who was beheaded at *Fothering-hay Castle*, some
say by the privity, others to the great discontent of Queen
Elizabeth : A Lady of a sharp wit, undaunted spirit, comely
person, Beautiful face, Majestick presence, a fluent Orator. and
an excellent Poet, as may appear by several things of her
writing now extant ; amongst others of her verses, this was one,
which she wrote with a pointed Diamond, in a window, during
her Imprisonment in *Fothering-hay Castle*.

> *From the top of all my trust,*
> *Mishap hath laid me in the dust.*

She was beheaded the 8*th* day of *February*, *Anno* 1587, and
was first buried in the Quire of *Peterborough*, afterwards by her
son King *James*, solemnly removed from thence to *Westminster*,
where in the South side of the Chappel of King *Henry* the
seventh. he erected a stately monument to her memory. The
following is an

[*Extract from the Burial Register of the Cathedral at Peterborough*]

The Queene of ⎫ 1587
Scots buried — ⎭ item

☞ The Queene of Scots was most sumptuously buried in the
Cathedrall Church of Peterborough, the first day of August, who
was for her derserts beheaded at Fotheringgay, about Sainte
Paule's day before ! Anthony More one of the Children of the
Queene's Maties Kitchen, who followed at the funerall aforesaid
of the Q. of S. was buried the iij day.

> *The Harp shall give a better sound.*

The Harp signifies *Ireland*, as being the Armes of that
Country, which *Queen Elizabeth* by reducing to a better obedience.
made it give a *better sound*, that is made it more civilized
and profitable to the Exchequer then ever before.

An Earl without a Head be found.

This was spoken of the Earl of *Essex*, one who was the favourite of the *Queen*, and darling of the people ; (two things which seldom come together), and yet could not both of them protect him from the Scaffold, but that thereon he lost his Head.

Soon after shall the English Rose,
Unto a Male, her place Dispose.

By the *English Rose*, is meant *Queen Elizabeth*, as we said before ; by whose Death. the Right and Title to the Crown, came to *James* the sixth, the King of *Scotland*, as lineally descended from *Margaret* the Eldest Daughter to King *Henry* the seventh ; the issue Male failing, by the Death of *Queen Elizabeth :* and here is to be remembered, the Policy of King *Henry* the seventh, who having two Daughters, Married the Eldest of them to King of *Scotland ;* and the youngest to the King of *France*, that if his issue Male should happen'd to fail (as it afterwards did) then *Scotland* might wait upon *England* as the greater Kingdom, and not *England* upon *France* as the lesser : Besides there was an old Prophesie, which intimated King *James* his coming to the *English* Crown ; for when King *Edward* the First haraced *Scotland*, amongst other things he brought from thence their Royal *Chair* (still preserved at the *Abbey* in *Westminster*) upon which *Chair* these verses were writ.

If Fates go right, where ere this Chare *is Pight,*
The Regal Race of Scots *shall rule that Place.*

Which by the Coronation of King *James* there performed, made good the words of the Prophesie.

CHAPTER XIII.

The Prophesies of the Reign of King James, *his uniting* England *and Scotland, his Peaceable Reign, a learned time, the Powder Treason ; the Marriage with the Prince Elector, and Lady* Elizabeth ; *the Death of Prince* Henry.

The Northern Lyon *over* Tweed,
The Maiden Queen shall then succeed,

And joyn in one, two mighty States,
Janus *then shall shut his Gates.*
Mars *shall yield to* Mercury,
All things tend to Prosperity.
Hells power by a fatal blow,
Shall seek the Land to overthrow.
Which by mistake shall be reverst,
And heads from shoulders be disperst.
The British Olive *next shall twine*
In marriage with the German *Vine.*
The Ninth to Death his power shall yield
Death conquers all, he winns the Field.

Next follows the remarkable actions of King *James's* Reign. predicted in the foregoing lines, which may be thus explained.

The Northern Lyon *over* Tweed,
The Maiden Queen shall then succeed,
And joyn in one, Two mighty States.

By the Northern *Lyon,* is meant King *James ;* and by the Maiden *Queen,* Queen *Elizabeth,* whom King *James,* being King of *Scotland* succeeded in the *English* Crown, joyned thereby the two Nations of *England* and *Scotland,* which had been often attempted before, not only by Conquest, but by Marriage ; once by Conquest, by King *Edward* the first, who subdued their strong places, and made their Nobles yield him obeisance; yet what they thus lost by him, they recovered of his son King *Edward* the second ; the other of Marriage, was by King *Henry* the eighth, who endeavoured to have matched his son, Prince *Edward,* with the Heiress of *Scotland,* and had proceeded very farr therein, when death cut him off; and though afterwards attempted by the Duke of *Somerset,* Lord Protector, and the *Scots* beaten at *Musselborough field,* yet all would not prevail ; God having decreed their union to be afterwards, in a more peaceable manner.

Janus *then shall shut his Gates.*

Janus was one of the gods belonging to the ancient *Romans ;* whose Temple was never shut, but in the daies of Peace, which happened not above twice, in the space of two thousand years : King *James* his Reign being a very peaceable time, when Swords rusted in their Sheathes for want of using them ; *Mother Shipton* in her Prophesie alludes thereto.

> Mars *shall yield to* Mercury,
> *All things tend to prosperity.*

War shall give place to Peace, fighting to pleading, the Sword to the Gown, the Pike to the Pen, Barbarism to Learning, &c., this Peace shall cause Plenty, Plenty work, prosperity, &c.

> *Hells Power by a fatal Blow,*
> *Shall seek the Land to overthrow.*
> *Which by mistake shall be reverst,*
> *And Heads from Shoulders be disperst.*

These Lines have reference to the horrid Powder Plot, which was to have been acted by some desperate Papists, to have blown up the Parliament House with Gun-powder, and therein out Religion, Laws, King, Prince, Peers, Bishops, Judges, Knights, and Burgesses, all designed to Destruction : The chief actors herein were, *Robert Catesby, Thomas Percy, Sir Edward Digby, Francis Tresham, Robert Winster, Thomas Winter, John Wright, Chris. Wright, Ambrose Rookwood, Robert Keys, John Graunt, Guido Fox,* and *Bates, Catesbies* man ; Gentlemen, most of Ancient Families. some of plentiful Fortunes. but all of resolute Spirits : These being suggested by the Devil, and seconded by his Agents, the Jesuits, to bring their purpose about, hire a Vault under the Parliament House, wherein they stowed Thirty-six Barrels of Powder. with several Iron barrs to make the force of the fire more effectual, all which they covered with Billets, thinking thereby to have covered their Design, from being Discovered : On the Fifth of November, the day of the Parliaments first sitting, was the time appointed to put their Design in execution : but Providence had ordered it otherwise, that those who intended mischief, should taste the effects of it ; on the Evening before, came to the Lord *Monteagle,* a strange Letter, from a strange hand, by a strange messenger ; without Date to it, name at it, and (to outward appearance) sense in it : A Letter which when it was opened, was even still Sealed, such the affected obscurity therein : The Letter contained these words.

My Lord,

Out of the Love I bear to some of your Friends, I have a care of your Preservation; therefore I would advise you, as you tender your Life, to devise some excuse, to shift off your attendance at this Parliament: *For God and Man have concurred to punish the wickedness of this time. And think not slightly of this Advertisement, but retire your self into your Country, where you may expect the Event in Safety: for though there be no appearance of any stir, yet I say, they shall receive a terrible blow this* Parliament, *and yet they shall not see who hurts them: This counsel is not to be Contemned, because it may do you good, and can do you on harm; for the danger is past so soon as you have burnt the Letter; and I hope God will give you the grace to make good use of it: to whose holy Protection I commend you.*

This Letter being communicated to the King, he expounded the mystical *Blow*, to be meant by Gun-powder, and thereupon commanded the Rooms under the *Parliament House* to be searcht, where the *Mystery of Iniquity* was quickly discovered, some of the Traytors taken in *London*, others in the Country; the hands of Justice overtaking them, they became examples of Justice, and tasted of that Cup (though not with that Cruelty) which they intended others should have drank of.

> *The British* Olive *next shall twine,*
> *Im marriage with the* German *Vine.*

By the *British Olive*, is meant the *Lady Elizabeth*, Daughter to King *James*; and by the *German Vine*, the most Illustrious Prince *Frederick, Count Palatine* of the *Rhine*; this Lady *Elizabeth* was enriched with all the endowments both of Body and mind, which make to the compleating of a Princess; most dearly beloved of the *English*, as one that deserved well of all; hear a wit of that age thus complaining—

> *Most sweet* Elizabeth ! *that happy Name,*
> *If we lost nothing else by losing thee,*
> *So dear to* England *is, we are to blame:*
> *If without tears and sights we parted be.*

They were married with great solemnity, at *Westminster February* 14, Anno 1612.

> *The Ninth to Death his Power shall yield.*
> *Death Conquers all, he wins the Field.*

This is meant of Prince *Henry*, who is here called the Ninth, in regard that if he had lived till King *James* dyed, he would have been the Ninth King of that name, since the Conquest : He was a Prince of most excellent parts, not wanting any thing wherewith Nature and Art could enrich him ; of a very Pious disposition, never heard by any alive to swear an Oath, for which *Arch-bishop Abbot* commended him in his Funeral Sermon, the Prince being wont to say, *That he knew no Game, or value to be wonne or lost, that could be worth an Oath.* He died of an extraordinary burning Feaver, being generally lamented of the whole Land.

CHAPTER XIV.

The Prophesies of the Reign of King Charles *the First, his Marriage with* France *; the Murther of the Duke of* Buckingham *; the Scottish Troubles ; of the Long Parliament, and Bloody War ensuing after ; the execrable Murther of the King.*

MOTHER SHIPTON having proceeded thus far in her Prophesies, broke off abruptly with a deep sigh, the tears trickling down her cheeks, accompanied with the wringing of her hands, as if some extraordinary mischance had befallen. The *Abbot* wondered greatly what should be the cause of this sudden alteration, having observed all along before a settled composedness in her countenance, and now to break out into such exclamations : He therefore thus said unto her, *Mother Shipton*, it is more than some ordinary matter which hath made you to break out into this sudden passion ; and if it may not be troublesome unto you, I shall desire, that as hitherto you have not been scrupulous in revealing those secrets unto me, which have wrought in me both wonder and amazement, so that now you will not so abruptly break off, as to leave me in suspense of the cause of your sorrow : *Ah Mr. Abbot* (said she) *who can with dry eyes repeat what must next ensue, or but think upon it without a heart full of Agony ; to see vertue trampled on, and vice exalted ; Begars on Horse-back, and Princes on foot ; the Innocent condemned, and the Blood-thirsty go scot-free ;* But since my promise binds me to fulfill your request, I shall proceed where I left.

> *The Crown then fits the White* Kings *Head,*
> *Who with the Lillies soon shall wed ;*
> *Then shall a Peasants bloody knife,*
> *Deprive a great Man of his Life.*
> *Forth from the* North *shall mischief blow,*
> *And* English *Hob shall add thereto.*
> *Then shall the Council great Assemble,*
> *Who shall make great and small to tremble.*
> Mars *shall rage as he were wood,*
> *And earth shall drunken be with blood.*
> *The White King then (O grief to see)*
> *By wicked Hands shall Murdered be.*

These lines are so plain, relating to the Actions of the late times, as shall need no *Oedipus* to explain them ; as we have all along before made several Comments upon her Text, we shall here likewise proceed in the same Method as we did before.

The Crown then fits the White Kings Head.

By the *White King* is meant King *Charles* the first, so called not only in respect of the purity and uprightness of his life, signified by White ; but also that at the time of his Coronation he was clothed in *White,* which some venomous tongues have since urged against him, that *he was not Crowned as other* Kings, as if Princes might not have the same liberty as meaner persons, to assume what coloured Garb they list to wear, to themselves.

Who with the Lillies soon shall wed.

Somewhat before *King James* his Death a marriage was concluded on betwixt Prince *Charles,* and the *Lady Henrietta Maria,* Daughter to that Martial Prince *Henry* the fourth. King of *France ;* but before the Consummation thereof, King *James* dyed, not long after his Funerals were over, she was brought into *England*, and solemnly married to King *Charles*, who is hereupon said to wed the *Lillies*; the *Lillies* being the Armes of *France*.

> *Then shall a Peasants bloody Knife,*
> *Deprive a great Man of his Life.*

This is spoken of the Duke of *Buckingham*, the greatest man in favour of those times, and thereupon (as it is most commonly seen) most hated of the People; who laid the blame of all miscarriages in the State upon him; right or wrong he was sure to undergo their censure: Being made General for the Relief of *Rochel* (then besieged by the *French* Forces) before he Imbarked at *Portsmouth*, he was most villanously Stabbed by one *Felton* a discontented Officer in his Army; who was so far from flying for the same, that though he might have passed away undiscovered, he boldly avowed himself to be the man that did it; alledging, that he had therein done his Country good service; but before his Death was better Principled, and made sensible of the heinousnes of the sin of Murther, recanting his former erronous Principles, and dying very Penitently, being hanged in Chains at *Portsmouth*, Anno 1627.

> *Forth from the* North *shall mischief blow,*
> *And* English Hob *shall add thereto.*

This Prophesie alludes to that ancient Proverb, *From the cold North, all ill comes forth;* and may be understood of our troubles commencing in 1639, taking their original rise from *Scotland*, and fomented by several Factious Spirits in *England*, the Dragon of Presbytery beginning then to appear in its own colours, the *Kirk* of *Scotland* having so high an opinion of its own purity, that it participated more of *Moses* his Platform in the *Mount*, than other Protestant Churches, being a *Reformed Reformation;* so that the practice thereof might be divertory to others, and she fit to give, not take; write, not receive Copies from any Neighbouring Church; desiring that all others were like unto them, *save only in their afflictions.* Hereupon they stood so high upon their pantoffles, that they refused the Common-prayer; disclaimed their Bishops, raised Tumults, and under the pretence of defending the *Scottish Kirk*, raised a War against the *English State;* the venom of which poyson so infected the veins of the *English*, who followed the *Scottish*

President, that it brake forth into a most bitter War, and ended not, but with the deaths of many thousands of people.

> *Then shall the Council great assemble*
> *Who shall make great and small to tremble.*

By the *great Council* is meant the long-lasting Parliament, so known to all posterity, for the remarkable transactions therein: It began *November* the 3d, 1640, and may more properly be said, to be the Parliament *that wrought wonders*, then that in the time of King *Henry* the Third, which had the same appellation. By them fell the wise *Strafford*, and Reverend *Laud*; by them was Episcopacy voted down, and Presbytery voted up, by them was the Common-prayer denyed, and the Directory exalted; they were the first that brought that strange Riddle into the World, that a man may fight for and against his King; by them was the Oath *Ex Officio* condemned, and the Covenant (far worse) applauded; in sum, by them was the Church and State turned topsey turvey; but this can not be reported of all amongst them, many of them hated their doings, dissented from them, and suffered by them.

> Mars *shall rage as he were wood,*
> And Earth *shall drunken be with Blood:*

To repeat all the Skirmishes, Fights and Battels that have happened betwixt the Kings and Parliaments Forces (here intended by this Prophesie) would of its self, require a Volume; in some of which, *viz.*, that at *Marston-moore*, eight thousand men were killed at a time, so that the Earth might well be said to be drunken with their Blood; and which is the more pity, this shed by *English* men of one Country, Citizens against Citizens, Neighbours against Neighbours, nay, one Kinsman against another, and prosecuted with the greatest fury and vigor that might be, according to that of the *Poet*.

> *The highest fury reigns in Civil warr,*
> *And Country-men in fight most cruel are.*

As was verified all along during our unnatural Civil War, none holding out with more obstinancy, fighting more eagerly, nor in the execution more Bloody than they.

> *The White King then (O grief to see)*
> *By wicked hands shall murthered be.*

Spoken concerning the Execrable Murther of that Pious
Prince King *Charles* the First, the most Renowned for Piety,
Prudence and Patience; of all his contemporary Princes
throughout the whole World; of whom when all is said that can
be spoken, yet doth all come farr short of his deserved praises:
I shall therefore sum up all with this Epitaph made on him by
a learned Pen.

> *He that can spel a Sigh, and read a Tear,*
> *Pronounce amazement, and accent wild Fear:*
> *Having all grief by Heart; He, only he,*
> *I sit to Write and Read thy Elegie.*
> *Unvalued* Charles! *thou art so hard a Text,*
> *Writ in one Age, not understood i'th Next.*

CHAPTER XV.

The Reign of King Charles *the second, the Usurpation of* Crom-
well; *the strange Confusion of a Democrital Government; the
Restauration of the King; the great Sickness; the Burning of
the City of* London

> *The White King dead, the Wolfe shall then*
> *With blood possess the* Lyons *den.*
> *But death shall hurry him away,*
> *Confusion shall awhile bear sway:*
> *But Fate to* England *shall restore,*
> *A King to Reign as heretofore.*
> *Mercy and Justice too, likewise,*
> *He in his time shall exercise.*
> *Great death in* London *shall be though;*
> *And Men on tops of Houses go.*

These Prophesies being all fulfilled in the
memory of man, and so well known unto the World,
we shall be the briefer in the explanation of them.

> *The White King dead, the Wolfe shall then*
> *With blood possess the* Lyons *den.*

By the White King (as we said before) is meant King *Charles* the First; and by the Wolf. *Oliver Cromwel* so termed by reason of his bloody disposition; that Beast being judged most greedy and ravenous of all others; and therefore fitly resembled to *Cromwel*, whose ambition was such, that he left no means unattempted, until he had got into the *Lyons den*, that is to say, until he had attained the sole Government; which being done, he then plucked the Stairs down by which he had mounted, turning the Rump out of dores, making them his Servants who had formerly been his Masters: exercising his cruelty upon the Cavaliers, which he deemed double Policy, as being thereby rid of his Enemies, and enriching his Coffers with their Wealth, though it were in effect but Murther and Robbery, and Proclaimed him to be a Blood-thirsty-Tyrant.

But Death shall hurry him away.

Very remarkable was the day in which the Protector dyed, being the Third of *September*, Anno 1658, wherein the wind was so violent, that it overthrew many Houses, tore up many Trees by the Roots, tumbled down Chimneys, and unreav'd Barns and Stables; but as it is a very ill *wind that blows none good*, so with all the hurt this wind did, it made some recompence in blowing this Bloody Tyrant away, which made the people so little sensible of their losses, that they thought their private harms not to stand in competition with this general good.

Confusion shall awhile bear sway.

Spoken in respect of the Confusion of Governments we then had: First, a Rump Parliament, then a Protector, next a Rump Parliament agen, then a Fools bauble, called a *Committee of Safety*, afterwards a Rump Parliament agen; now thus, then that, a great many Governments, and none good.

But Fate to England *shall restore,*
A King to Reign, as heretofore.

This was fulfilled in the happy Restoration of King *Charles* the Second, which put a period to all those Oligarchical Confusions, and Restored the Land to its Ancient pristine Government; which till then, groaned under the pressures of a Company of Mechanical (and therein the worst sort of) Tyrants.

Mercy and Justice too likewise,
He in his time shall exercise.

Of this many are the examples which might be produced ;
how many, though notorious Delinquents, received to Mercy ?
Life given to those, who would have taken his life away ; few
only suffering, but such whose offences were so Capital as could
not come well within the Verge of a Pardon, or stood upon
Justification of their former execrable Actions : Such rotten
members deserving to be cut off from the body of the Common-
wealth, who otherwise would have been very obnoxious and
prejudicial to those that were found.

Great Death in London *shall be though.*

Verified by the great Plague in *London,* 1665 (which for
number), was the greatest that hath been known in these later
Centuries of years ; and which (if not any thing else) might
convince our Sectaries, how necessary that prayer in the Letany
is for to be used, *From Plague, Pestilence, and Famine, good
Lord deliver us.*

And men on tops of Houses go.

This was suddenly fulfilled in that great Conflagration of Fire,
which happened in *London,* Sept. 2, 3, and 4, *Anno* 1666, by
which so many Houses were destroyed, that men afterwards in
the Ruines, went on the tops of those Houses, whose lofty
Structures not long before, seemed to brave the skie, and which
would dazle weak eyes to look up and behold the tops of them.

☞ *Here follow other Prophesies she uttered, which
because they concern Future times, we shall leave to the
Interpretation of the Intelligent Reader.*

I.

The Fiery Year as soon as 'ore,
Peace shall then be as before.
Plenty every where is found,
And Men with Swords shall plow the Ground.

II.

The Time shall come, when Seas of Blood,
Shall mingle with a greater Flood.

III.

Great noise there shall be heard, Great Shouts and Cries.
And Seas shall Thunder, lowder than the Skyes,
Then shall three Lyons *fight with three and bring,*
Joy to a People, Honour to their King.

This *Mother Shipton*, the Author of these, and the foregoing Prophesies, Lived till she was of an extraordinary Age; and though she was generally believed to be a witch, yet all persons what ever, that either saw, or heard of her, had her in great esteem: and her memory to this day is much honoured by those of her own Country.

A stone was erected near *Clifton*, about a Mile from the city of *York*, from which the following is taken.

𝔈𝔭𝔦𝔱𝔞𝔭𝔥.

𝔥𝔢𝔯𝔢 𝔩𝔶𝔢𝔰 𝔰𝔥𝔢 𝔴𝔥𝔬 𝔫𝔢𝔳𝔢𝔯 𝔩𝔶'𝔡,
𝔚𝔥𝔬𝔰𝔢 𝔰𝔨𝔦𝔩𝔩 𝔬𝔣𝔱𝔢𝔫 𝔥𝔞𝔰 𝔟𝔢𝔢𝔫 𝔱𝔯𝔶'𝔡,
𝔥𝔢𝔯 𝔓𝔯𝔬𝔭𝔥𝔢𝔠𝔦𝔢𝔰 𝔰𝔥𝔞𝔩𝔩 𝔰𝔱𝔦𝔩𝔩 𝔰𝔲𝔯𝔳𝔦𝔳𝔢,
𝔞𝔫𝔡 𝔢𝔳𝔢𝔯 𝔨𝔢𝔢𝔭 𝔥𝔢𝔯 𝔫𝔞𝔪𝔢 𝔞𝔩𝔦𝔳𝔢.

FINIS.